IN SEARCH
OF TRUTH

In Search of Truth

Finding solutions to life's riddles

Dr. Prashant Kakoday

Jupitarian Publishing

Published by Jupitarian Publishing

ISBN 978-1-7399466-0-9

Typesetting services by BOOKOW.COM

To BapDada for being the source of these ideas and for your continued guidance.

PREFACE

The seed for this publication to come into fruition was planted in the early 1990's, at a seminar in Hamburg, Germany, where concepts from this book were presented for the first time. Professor Reinhard Tausch, from the department of Psychology at Hamburg university, approached me to ask whether the ideas being presented had been written in the form of a book. When shared that they had not, he stated his view of the importance of them being captured in a written format. This conversation sparked the beginning of this book.

Over the next couple of years, the teachers and students associated with the Cambridge Meditation Centre would continue to discuss and experiment with these ideas. This collective churning led to beautiful experiences that gave a deeper meaning to the spiritual process. Up to this point in time, we were just students who knew there was something special here but had limited personal experiences. This process led many to experience that jump or shift into the beyond, with clear insights into what exists on the other side. The results of our churning and experiences were captured in written form in a publication titled 'God's Wisdom', which was released in limited circulation, mainly to students of Raj Yoga.

Years later, while visiting Ho Chi Minh City in Vietnam, a very nice incident occurred that highlighted the meaningful impact that the limited publication had on some. One lady approached me asking if I would be able to visit her father in the hospital who was possibly terminal and quite eager to meet me. She explained that she had received a copy of the limited publication and shared it with her father. As her father had worked with Americans in Vietnam earlier in his life, he had a good command over the English language. Seeing its immense value, he took it upon himself to translate the book into Vietnamese to a level that it was published and sold in book shops - making Vietnam the only country that it was sold in book shops. When I met with her father in the hospital, it was such a pleasure to hear him explain the story behind his personal experiences and progress. He primarily wanted to translate the publication for his daughter to gain a better understanding of the concepts but consequently, it had also reached many others in the country.

Over time, our understanding and experiences at the subtle level have continued to evolve and deepen. However, the decision was made to publish this book in line with how it naturally evolved many years ago. Subsequent publications will follow that will help readers build upon the ideas presented in this book. This book has been renamed 'In Search of Truth' to highlight that knowledge and insight serve as a powerful medium for deep spiritual experiences. Many other experiences will follow, however realisation itself is a necessary experience that must be acknowledged before it can be built upon.

The ideas presented in this book are inspired by the murlis studied daily by Raj Yoga students of the Brahma Kumaris. An attempt is made to have a rational discussion on the ideas often covered in a seven-day course offered at Brahma Kumari centres across the world. This publication also introduces a chapter on 'time' which may appear abstract, within the already abstract subject of spirituality. However, it can serve as a useful model that may help us see the physical world in a completely new way and offer a better understanding of the concept of time - from a scientific point of view.

ACKNOWLEDGMENTS

The first and foremost acknowledgement I would like to give is to the students of our BK centre in Cambridge. It was a joy to be part of the process of collective exploration and experimentation of the ideas that we learnt every morning.

I am very grateful to Sheila Eiloart, for her all round support and typing up of the first edition on an early Macintosh computer. I would like to thank those who supported with their editing skills and dedication especially Belinda Westcott and the late Barbara Heffer. Thanks to Heather Kara for her initative in getting In Search of Truth to it's present digital format and to Sarah FitzGerald for her all round skills and completing this edition with Jupitarian publishing. I extend my gratitude to many others who contributed to the creation process in various ways.

A special mention to Manolo from Barcelona for his illustrations and Judi Rich for the cover design.

CONTENTS

Chapter 1

MESSAGE OF NATURE

Nature's Ways

If there is anything that has fascinated mankind over the ages, it is the wonder with which nature's laws operate in the universe. To discover that there are a few simple laws behind the apparent complexities of matter with its various patterns has been Man's greatest satisfaction. In practice, we see that these laws exist and apply to everything around us, including us. Whatever happens in the world happens within the framework of these laws - some known to us, some unknown.

There are various laws described in physics e.g. the law of gravity, the laws of thermodynamics, etc. There are various laws in chemistry; there are laws for metabolic and physiological processes.

We can also observe a tendency in nature to sustain or to preserve. If something is thrown up into the air, it will be brought to the earth again and certain stability will be achieved. If a person cuts his finger, the laws of physiology will act on the wound until it is brought back to normal. We can take innumerable examples and see how the earth and the world have been sustained by these laws of nature. If we look around and see that there are rocks and birds and plants and human beings and all have existed for thousands of years, it is because of nature's tendency to sustain.

We can make a basic premise that nature is our friend and plays a role to sustain, to preserve or to stabilise life and matter. It has its own order of priorities, and given the choice, it may opt to preserve the higher in preference to the lower e.g. to preserve the species in preference to the individual, or to preserve the body in preference to the part (the cells of the body are constantly destroyed and re-placed to achieve a higher purpose of preserving the body). Based on this premise, we deduce that if there are circumstances where we just see the destructive side of nature, it is because we have not understood its role of sustaining a higher cause.

Price of Free Will

We can observe with great wonder how these tendencies in nature sustain the entire animal, plant and mineral kingdoms. Roots will naturally be drawn towards water; leaves will naturally face the sun; human intestines will secrete the right type of digestive juices specific to the food ingested, and so on. Sustenance takes place involuntarily. But, when it comes to animals with their own 'will', we come to a new situation. They possess a very special ability compared to plants and that is free will. They can take decisions and act. But, these abilities in isolation, could allow the animal to unintentionally harm itself. For example, it could go into a fire and burn, or a man could cut his finger and bleed without being aware of what had happened. So, in nature, free will is balanced by the phenomenon of pain and this combination yields sustenance.

So humans, as well as animals, experience pain from anything that is potentially dangerous; pain from heat, pain from sharp objects, pain from a wrong posture, pain from abnormal strain on muscles or ligaments, etc. If a person treads on a pin or is about to tread on a pin, the sharp pain from the pin gives him a warning, a message, and this helps him to protect his foot. The pain will persist or increase until he understands the message and pays attention to the danger.

Therefore, with animals and human beings alike, pain sensation exists solely to guard against the misuse of free will. This is clearly demonstrated in the anatomy of the human body. There are sensory receptors for pain in areas where we have voluntary control, but in areas of the body where there is no voluntary control, those particular pain receptors are conspicuously absent, e.g. the intestines. (A surgeon can dissect and cut out a few yards of intestines with a scalpel, without any pain to the patient. Anaesthesia is required only because of the pain from the skin incision.) It is our common experience that if we take something intolerably hot in the mouth and if we swallow it, the same heat experienced in the mouth is not experienced in the oesophagus or stomach. Heat and pain sensations exist only up to the cricopharynx, which is also the limit of voluntary control over the muscles. In essence, the sensation of pain guides our free will and has an important message aimed at protecting against harm.

Decoding the Message

If we realize the wisdom of Nature and also understand the significance of the pain phenomenon, it leads us to certain important conclusions:

1. There is a message in every pain that we experience and we should therefore not suppress pain without understanding the message behind it.

2. For the more complex types of pain (in the form of illnesses) interpretation of the message may be difficult, therefore more effort must be made to understand these messages. For example the relationship between joint pains and the wrong type of diet may be difficult to decode or interpret. Nevertheless, that is the way nature speaks!

3. Messages exist behind emotional pain and mental suffering, e.g. sadness, frustration, etc. Just as physical pain disappears once the message is understood and appropriate steps are taken, in the same way, all emotional suffering would disappear if we understand the message accurately and take appropriate steps to remove the cause.

The Message of Emotional Suffering

It is not a virtue to suffer emotionally, whether it is just a temporary malaise or a more severe depression. To remove the suffering it is important for us to understand the message behind it and bring about appropriate changes. If the lesson is not learnt, the suffering will linger on, or will increase until attention is paid and the necessary changes brought about.

The emotional pain or reaction can be very different in different individuals under apparently identical circumstances. If a glass half-filled with juice is offered to two individuals, one may be pleased to see the glass half-filled and the other may be sad to see that the glass is half-empty. When the weather forecasters expect a hurricane to hit a particular state, some spend their time waiting anxiously, whilst others organise 'Hurricane parties' and prepare 'Hurricane punch'!

Factors for human emotional suffering are not all external, such as a hurricane. One important factor is very much within us and is associated with our inner make-up or personality. We shall call this the 'human factor' and explore it in a little more detail.

Chapter 2

WHO AM I?

The Existing World

Before we discuss the subject of 'Who am I?' it is appropriate for us to understand some of our fundamental limitations in knowing about the existing world.

In figure 1, the whole of the existing world is represented by the vertical straight line from A to B.

Let us imagine certain caterpillars exist who have only one sense organ, the sense of touch. They don't have a sense of smell, hearing or vision, and their entire understanding of reality is based on the information they receive through the sense of touch. For such an organism, the manifest world is limited to the segment of line from A - C, and it cannot know, for instance, of the moon and stars. They perhaps have their own reductionist scientists who have ongoing arguments as to whether there is a moon or not!

In the same way, certain reptiles don't have ears and for them, so-called music or noise doesn't exist. Bats don't have vision and so some distant clouds don't exist for them and they are limited to experiencing the segment from A - D. However, we know that the

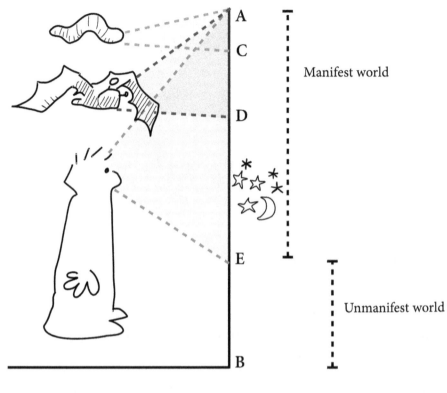

Figure 1

existing world is not limited to the number of senses that the cater-pillar or the bat has.

With human beings, we have five senses; sight, smell, hearing, taste and touch. Through these senses we receive information of the world around us, but just as the existing world is not limited to those things that the bat can sense, in the same way, there is no rea-son to suppose that the existing world is limited to those things that human beings can sense. In fact, over the past 100 years or so, we have been able to learn a lot more about the existing world that is un-manifest to the human senses. For example, our eyes can't de-tect x-rays, our ears can't detect even loud sounds if they are above 18,000Hz frequency and we are unable to detect the signals used by homing pigeons and migrating birds that enable them to navigate thousands of miles and arrive at their precise destination.

All this leads us to one conclusion, that there is more in the world than is perceived through our five senses. The part of the existing world that cannot be perceived by human beings is described as the un-manifest world, whereas the other that can be perceived is known as the manifest world. The entire field of science has to restrict itself to the manifest world because of its methodology based on sense perception. Any institution with such limitations cannot offer us a true picture of reality or can be relied upon to provide the solutions to human or world problems.

When we come to the question of 'Who am I?' science is incapable of providing a satisfactory answer, so it is necessary to investigate alternative sources. In fact, it is more urgent or important than we realise since suffering has a direct connection with our knowledge or ignorance of the subject.

Travelling along the path to 'know ourselves' is a very personal affair. We have to rely on our own experiences and our own observations, and since only we can observe our own minds, it is an individual search. It is essentially an empirical approach with our minds as laboratories. As we go further through this book, it is hoped that you will experiment with the various ideas, check them with your past experiences, test them in the laboratory of the mind and refine them through your own reasoning.

Who Am I?

Having considered some of the limitations of perception, let us return to the question 'Who am I?' We shall use the expression 'Real

I' for the entity that we are looking for. One of the definite properties of the 'Real I' is the ability to experience. Just as different parts
and organs of the body have different functions, the 'Real I' has the
function to experience. It is the experiencer. When I say, 'I am in
this room' it is because the 'Real I' is experiencing this room.

Let us take an example of the eighty year-old man who says he
exists today. He also says he remembers his childhood when he
was 5 years old. He says he is the same person who lived more
than 75 years ago… he existed then. (See Figure 2.)

Figure 2

First of all, let us try and understand whether 'he' belongs to the
manifest world or the un-manifest world. First, let us take the possibility of the manifest world. The body which he had 75 years ago
has not only changed in shape and size, but we cannot expect a single atom that was present then to exist now. The rate of tissue re-

placement in the body is so rapid, that some of the cells are replaced within days. Others, like skin cells, are replaced within weeks and bones within years, whilst the micro-molecular mass of the brain is replaced within 3 days. (The nerve cell may remain the same, but all its molecules will get replaced.) Every minute we breathe in and out several litres of air. Oxygen and nitrogen from air become part of our bodies and body molecules are expelled, and this process is continuous. So, over a period of 75 years, the molecules and cells, i .e., the material, the manifest body, is replaced many times. Whatever can be dissected and seen under the microscope in his present body was not part of his body seventy-five years ago.

If nothing from the manifest body of a 5 year-old boy continues into the body when he is 80 years old, then the 'Real I' which continues over those 75 years can't belong to the manifest body and the manifest world. This means it has to belong to the un-manifest world. So, we can say that one of the characteristics of the 'Real I' is that it is un-manifest or non-physical, i.e. beyond the perception of the five human senses.

This is not the first time that we are realising our non-physical nature. We may not use the words but we accept the continuity of the person, in spite of the physiological knowledge of the changing physical body. Even the law believes in the continuity of the non-physical 'Real I'. Let us consider a person who is found guilty of a crime which he committed several years earlier. Even if he was to prove that he had had liver, heart and kidney transplants or even that his entire physical body was different since the crime, he would still be found guilty. The one who is convicted is the 'Real I', the 'non-physical experiencer'.

Out of Body Experiences

Miss S. Mackay, from Cambridge had repeated Out of Body experiences from childhood. The following is her personal account: 'As a child, I often saw myself outside the body. It was as if my consciousness was outside, at a much higher level looking down on myself. As I grew, I realised that others didn't have similar experiences and so I was reluctant to speak about them. During my teens I would get these experiences when I was not comfortable. For example, one day my father was hosting a dinner for his diplomat friends. I saw the artificiality of the interactions. Soon, I saw myself far away at a high position looking at the scene from above. I can't have these experiences voluntarily. More recently, they have become much less frequent. When I am outside the body, I can see the unnecessary importance that I give to trivial situations. All so called problems appear trivial. They still remain, but my attitude towards them changes. I remain calm, free from anxiety and conflict.'

When we understand the reality of the 'Real I' there is a sensible explanation for the phenomena of Out of body experiences.

The Experience and the Experiencer

The understanding that the 'Real I' is different from the body infers the possibility of the existence of the 'Real I' beyond the death of the body and possible immortality. Can eternity or immortality be proved? The word 'eternal' is used where the entity has no beginning or end. When one undertakes the task to prove something not to exist, the maximum evidence that we can produce is that it is not seen to exist. For example, in order to establish that there is no chair in a room, all we can do is to show that the chair is not seen in the room. An entity called 'no chair' does not exist which could be produced as evidence of the chair's non-existence. In the same way, if an entity is thought to have no beginning and no end, the corresponding evidence for that would be when we cannot see the beginning or the end of the entity. (See Figure 3.)

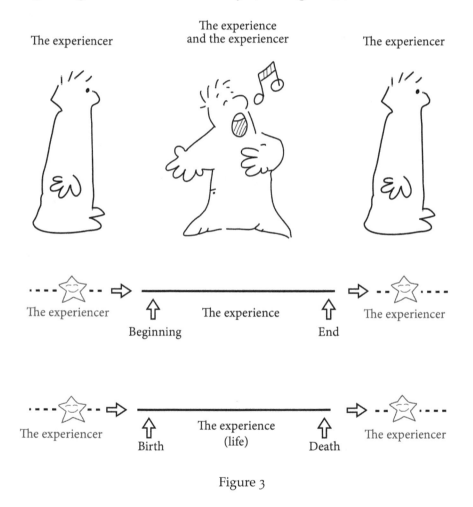

Figure 3

We said earlier that one of the principal functions of the 'Real I' is to experience. It is important to distinguish between the 'experience' and the 'experiencer'. The description of the experiencer is

13

different from that of the experience, just as the listener is different from a song he listens to. Every experience, by definition, has a beginning and an end. For example, a man touches a pen; that is the beginning of an experience, and the moment he stops touching the pen, it is the end of the experience. A person may enter a room and after a time leave again, an observer can only conclude that there was a beginning and an end to the person's experience of the room, and cannot determine the beginning or end of the experiencer. So, 'a beginning and an end' is certainly a description of an experience, but that does not tell us about the beginning and the end of the experiencer.

All that we know about birth and death is that we have the beginning and end of a very long experience. By the same token, we cannot conclude the end of the experiencer who left the room, even with the death of the body, we cannot conclude the demise of the 'Real I'.

Various medical and scientific observations support this inference. For instance, there are thousands of recorded cases, worldwide, where patients have been declared dead and remained 'dead' for several minutes or even hours, but suddenly returned to life. In many cases, death certificates had been signed and the bodies sent to the mortuary. But, when these individuals returned to life, they related experiences of being outside the body, often termed the 'Near Death Experience' (NDE). Some experienced a dark tunnel and some experienced viewing their body from outside. The experiencer was very much alive, and was experiencing different scenes: the 'Real I' was not dead. To date, there is not a single shred of medical or scientific case evidence to support the view that with the death of the body the experiencer ceases to exist; yet we consistently consider ourselves to be mortal without any basis of experience, reason, logic or evidence.

The 'Real I' and the Brain

Without clear understanding of the nature of the 'Real I', people have wrongly attributed many of the functions of the 'Real I' to the brain and nervous system, including the function of experiencing itself.

When we use the word 'brain' we are referring to a mass of nerve cells and connective tissue cells, covered by membranes; a very material entity. Science has explored all manner of possible properties of matter, but so far, no-one has hypothesised that matter has the capacity to experience. It seems highly improbable from our own experience as well, if it were otherwise, our shoes and chairs would have regularly complained! If matter cannot experience, then how can the brain, which is made of matter, experience.

The brain can and does, however, perform various material functions; its cells transfer messages as electrical signals, record and store information. Like a computer, the brain coordinates the complex movements of the body and so on. The brain carries out many important functions in the body, but only those of a physical nature. It is the non-physical 'Real I' alone which has the role of the experiencer.

Another of the important functions within us - decision making - is based totally upon comparing current options with past experience, and so can be performed only by the one who experiences. Therefore decision-making, (discriminating or choosing) also belongs to the 'Real I'.

Just as computers or cars can perform many complex functions, but require an operator, matter at best, can be the instrument to be used by the one who can decide. In the same way, the brain which is made up of matter is a superb instrument for the use of the one who is able to decide. Thus the brain (and in turn, the body) are instruments operated and controlled by the 'Real I'. To a large degree, decision making is carried out through the medium of thought, therefore 'thinking' occurs within the 'Real I' as well.

Each thought is associated with certain feelings or emotions and so these also emerge from the 'Real I'. Therefore, we can see that the 'Real I' carries out all cognitive functions. We have also seen that the brain happens to be the immediate instrument, like the control room through which the 'Real I' operates. It would be the task of neurophysiologists to research and find out the exact level of interaction of this non-physical 'Real I' with the physical neurotransmitters and the electrical states of brain cells. It is the 'Real I' that receives information of the physical world through the senses via the brain and it, in turn, executes its decisions through the brain in order to use the body to perform actions.

So far, we have mentioned that the 'Real I' is un-manifest and performs these various subtle functions. To be more specific, having seen the various subtle functions performed by the 'Real I', such as decision-making, thinking, feeling, etc, we can describe the 'Real I' as a 'Being' of very subtle life energy or as a Being of subtle light. One way to describe an un-manifest entity is as an infinitesimally small point. Thus the un-manifest 'Real I' can be seen as an infinitesimally small point of subtle light.

If the 'Real I' is the ruler of this body, using the brain as the control room, then there is no place better than the brain or the hypothalamus, to be more precise, from where it can efficiently control both hemispheres of the cerebrum, cerebellum, pituitary, endocrines and the autonomic nervous system, and thus virtually every cell of the whole body. The hypothalamus is immediately behind the centre of the forehead, in between the two eyebrows.

So, if we were to look for a physical location for the 'Real I', a point in the forehead, in between the two eyebrows, would be a fair bet.

The First Illusion: 'My' and 'Mine'

One of the earliest errors in our 'belief system' is the belief of ownership. Figure 4 shows the exposure of the 'Real I' to the physical world from birth to death. In comparison to the eternal existence of the 'Real I', one million years are insignificant. A full lifespan, say of 100 years in the physical body and in the physical world is even more insignificant. Certainly, with that limited exposure, it doesn't own those physical entities. When it leaves the body at death, it cannot carry a single atom from this world with it. The law and society may even accept that the 'Real I' owns certain property, but the next day, if it were to leave the body, (i.e. to die) it couldn't take anything with it. This is the clear view of our relationship with this world. If we were to enter a certain showroom for 5 minutes, we would not believe that anything there belonged to us.

In the same way, our true attitude towards these bodies and the world is that we do not own anything. We are the experiencers.

We have already mentioned that it is quite possible for the whole world to believe in something that is totally wrong and suffer as a result. We live in a global society where the systems, customs, laws etc. are based on a belief in ownership. Everyone believes that he or she owns certain things, and many are working flat out in the belief that they can own more. It has to be emphasised however, that we should not seek to escape from our bodies nor the physical objects around us, and that there is nothing wrong in using them, so long as we maintain the attitude of being a trustee of those things. Only

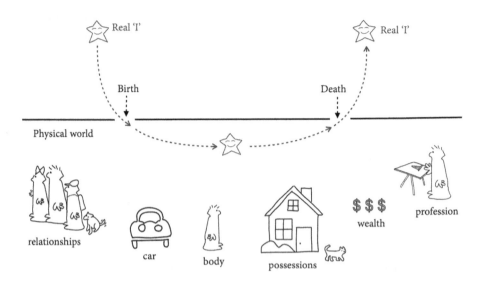

Figure 4

when we start to believe that we own things, do we break natural laws and therefore cause ourselves suffering.

There are a variety of reasons for believing that we own things. Common reasons are 'I use it', 'no-one else owns it', 'I bought it', 'I've been given it', 'I saw it first', etc. It is amazing to realise that the laws of countries are based on this same reasoning and just as children often quarrel using the word 'My', countries also quarrel with the same word 'My' for equally ridiculous beliefs.

In one study, a psychologist recorded the conversations of people to find out how often they use the words 'I', 'me', 'my' and 'mine' in fifteen minutes. There was one group who used these four words more than 118 times. A follow-up of these people over the next 10 years showed that the incidence of death amongst them due to myocardial infarction was much higher than for the others. The word 'my' could be quite lethal!

Let us see how the emotional state of a person can be affected by his belief in ownership. Consider the example of Mr X, who has £10 million, and Mr Y, who has just £100. Let's presume that both are in a state of peace at the moment. Now suppose Mr X loses £9 million pounds and is left with just £1 million. Mr Y continues to have only £100. Mr X still has 10,000 times more wealth than Mr Y, but what will be his emotional state now? It will certainly be far from peaceful. Just the fear of potentially losing his millions is enough to cause Mr X severe anxiety. Peace in a person is not related to what he owns, but it is certainly related to what he has lost, or may lose!

In our society, right from birth, the 'Real I' is made to enter into the labyrinth of 'my'. Mr X is representative of our present society. To start with, he feels he owns 'his' body, 'his' possessions, 'his' relations e.g. 'his' children. He continues to use these magic words 'my' and 'mine' to organisations, colleges, ideas, opinions, concepts, qualities, images and so on. He becomes an eclectic with a large empire of 'my'. He even defines himself in terms of these objects. (See Figure 5.)

Let us take an example of Mr B, in identical circumstances to Mr X, but he defines himself as a non-physical, eternal being, 'Real I' who doesn't own anything and uses the body and other physical objects, that are temporarily at his disposal, as a trustee. Mr X, being an eclectic, will feel 'I can lose everything' or, 'I have lost something', while Mr B will feel 'I can't lose anything'. This expression and feeling is the key to deep inner peace and security. (See Figure 6.)

Original Experience

So far we have introduced two fundamental realities: that the 'Real I' is un-manifest and that the 'Real I' is eternal. As the concepts of

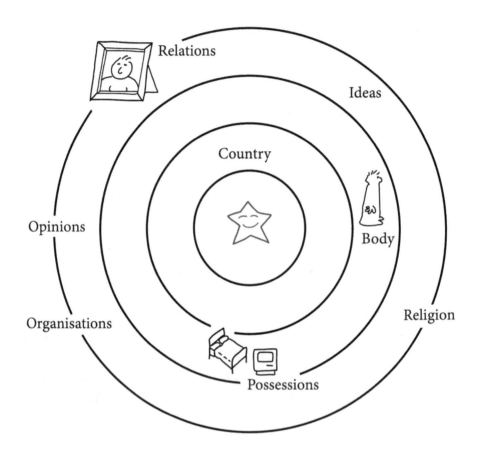

Figure 5

the un-manifest world and eternity are not discussed in any depth in everyday life, it is understandable that we won't find it easy to comprehend the implications of these concepts at first sight. The purpose of the present exercise is to open the mind to these new ways of thinking, with new possibilities and new horizons where we can exercise our intellects. The ultimate proof in these areas has to be discovered by each individual through his own realisations. The experience of these realisations can be hastened by taking steps to prepare our intellects to understand these concepts.

Once we realise that as non-physical beings we cannot lose any-

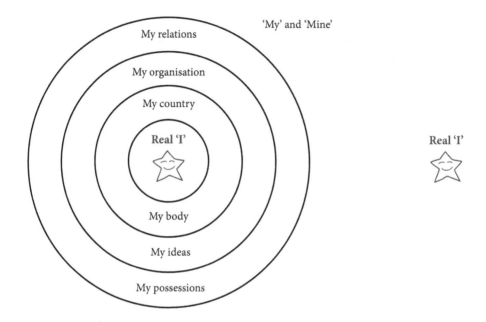

Figure 6

thing, this becomes the basis of deep inner security and inner peace. The realisation that we are eternal is not essential to the experience of inner security, but it helps to enrich it. The truth is: 'Come what may, I exist;' 'What I truly have, no one can take away from me;' 'I am different from this body, and even when the body dies I continue to exist;' 'Everyone else is also eternal and truly no-one dies;' 'What I am, I remain;' 'I do not own anything, and so I cannot lose anything.' This experience of security frees us from lots of unnecessary desires, (selfish small desires), and this, in turn, brings a sense of freedom. The more we are free from desires, the more there is contentment and we find ourselves in peace.

Peace comes with its friends. Along with peace comes the experience of joy and compassion. This experience of eternity, security, total freedom from desires, contentment, peace, compassion, love and joy, can be referred to as our 'Original Experience'. This was the experience when we were in the true awareness of ourselves – awareness of the 'Real I'. As we go through life, for various reasons we lose the truth about ourselves and with that, our original experience. All our efforts in life - as kings or beggars - are to return to that original experience. Just as water is the natural original environment for a fish and it will be uncomfortable the moment it is taken into the air, in the same way, for the 'Real I' - a state of peace, joy, love, compassion and contentment is the original natural environment. It is comfortable in that state. The moment it comes into anger, distress, envy, stress etc. there is inner discomfort and it struggles to come back into peace. Each and every human being is constantly pre-occupied with experiencing joy, compassion, peace and security. Each one tries in the way he thinks best for himself, but unless the effort is made at the level of the 'Real I,' there won't be that true, original experience.

T.S. Elliot says in the 'Quartets':

> We shall not cease from exploration
> And the end of all our exploring
> Will be to arrive where we started
> And know the place for the first time.

Once we experienced the highest state of constant peace, joy and compassion, but in time, we lost this original, highest experience. Our subsequent exploration has been to re-experience what we innately know is attainable, but we have sought to achieve this through material possessions and satiation of the senses. Now, having explored everywhere, it is time to come back to where we started - to return to our original state - the knowledgeful state. It is a journey which will lead us back to that highest experience.

A meditation experience
www.cambridgeinnerspace.org/med-1

Chapter 3

THE SMRITI

Awareness

We carry out many functions. We can see in ourselves that we can move the body, we can create thoughts, we can feel emotions etc. Some functions are very obvious to us and even to others, such as physical movements. Some others, like thoughts and emotions, are not so obvious to others, but are obvious to ourselves.

There is yet another important function within us, which is more subtle than thoughts and it is called awareness. It is distinct from thought and we will best understand it if we attempt to observe it whilst reading about it.

Right now, we are busy in various actions e.g. reading. Yet, we are also aware of the town or country we are residing in at the moment. It is not a conscious thought, nevertheless the awareness is there as to our orientation in space. Similarly, we have an awareness based on time. We know whether it is morning, evening, or night. We also have an awareness based on where we have come from and where we are going (e.g. come from home and going to a certain shop). Most of the time, we are not paying attention to these factors and the function of awareness is taking place in the background. Occasionally, we are consciously aware of the place, time, or sensations. In addition, these awarenesses may be based on correct or incorrect information. A person who has grossly abnormal or incorrect awareness of place or time, is a sign of mental ill health. When one loses some forms of awareness altogether, it's a sign of losing consciousness as in a case of head injury.

There is yet another type of awareness, in which we are particularly interested, and that is the awareness of who we are! We will notice that we also carry a certain description of ourselves in our awareness. This particular awareness is a very important function for human beings to study and we shall call this awareness by a Sanskrit word, 'Smriti'.

Smriti is a certain image about ourselves in our minds. The image may change with different circumstances and typically does so several times within an hour. It is a subtle function and so most of the time we may not be conscious of which one is in play. A lot of the time it may be based on the appearances of the body, (shape, size or dress) whilst at other times it may be based on our job, relationships, status or role. Whether someone consciously has ever asked the question 'Who am I?' or not, we all constantly carry our own answer to that question. It is not an intellectual answer because the majority of us may never intellectualise this subject. Even if intellectuals or philosophers were to consider the question 'Who am I?' their clever answer may be one thing, and their Smriti, in practice, may be something else.

Now is perhaps a good opportunity to observe the function of smriti in ourselves. What 'Smriti' am I in at this very moment? What is the image with which I see myself? How would I introduce me to myself, or how would I describe myself? How do I think of myself? Who am I? Do I see myself in terms of the body's physical appearance, in a certain dress, posture, or in a certain profession? Or is the 'Smriti' based on certain possessions, such as the owner of a smart sports car or smart house? Or is the 'Smriti' based on other people such as 'mother' or 'wife' of so and so? To be able to observe this function in ourselves impartially is the first major milestone on our journey.

The True Smriti

Imagine a person, who sits out in the garden under an apple tree. Just because he is associated with the tree, he doesn't call himself a tree. We have already discussed the fact that we are eternal, peaceful, conscient beings of subtle light. As our only true identity, we should be in this Smriti of 'Real I' all the time. There is no reason for any other Smriti at any time. This being of light, the 'Real I', finds itself in the physical world in association with many physical entities. It is associated with a body, it is born in a certain country, to a certain family and a certain race and so on. It is associated with the physical world for a short time - the 'Real I' may leave the whole scene at any time. Now, even as the 'Real I' travels through these physical associations, it remains the same 'Real I' - it remains an eternal, peaceful point of light.

To consider oneself even to be male or female, means the Smriti is being based upon the body and not on the 'Real I'. Male or female is the description of the body, and to consider oneself to be male or female, young or old, would appear strange. The 'Real I' is a totally different entity, and there is only one right Smriti.

Although our original state is one of constant peace, joy and compassion, we know that the human state is far from this now... so, where did we go wrong?

Let us follow the inevitable fate of this beautiful and peaceful 'Real I'... With its birth in the body, the 'Real I' is given bodily associations - a body, a name, relations, etc. In time, it associates with other factors such as profession, status, nationality, religion, car, etc. When the 'Real I' is associated with these things over a period of time, the 'Real I' begins to identify with these associations so, gives birth to Smritis based on external factors such as the body, objects, other people, social-status, and so on. We saw earlier how the 'Real I' believes that it owns things; to identify with external factors is a step yet further into illusion. So we find these 'Real I's' considering themselves to be bodies, men or women, English or French. He may consider himself to be a professor, another may consider himself to be a father. These are all examples of false Smriti's which bring the greatest suffering to human beings. An individual typically possesses dozens of false Smritis, all of which are competing for dominance of the mind. Henceforth, we shall use the word identity instead of Smriti and represent the true Smriti with a capital letter 'I' and false Smriti with the lower case 'i'. (See Figure 7.)

The Power of Collective Delusion

Often in life we find ourselves in a situation where we have erroneous information about a topic. In some cases we may know that the information is suspect, or just plain wrong. In many cases however, we may not know that it is in error, and may not even suspect any likelihood that it is not true. The problem is exacerbated if the erroneous belief is widely held to be true by everyone around you.

In this state of collective delusion, the right information will appear wrong and so no one can help anyone. False identity is one such

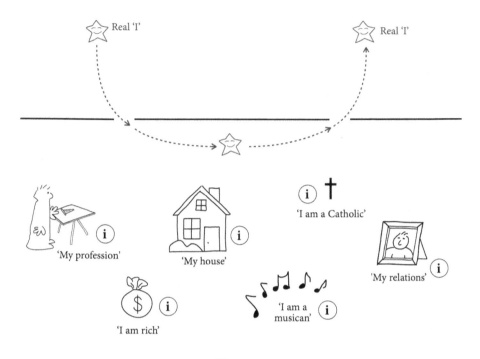

Figure 7

example. We are all convinced that we are these bodies, or our professions and never consider ourselves to be anything like the 'Real I'. The thought of being a secure, eternal being of light seems to be imagination and weird in the extreme. Nevertheless, when we realise these false identities are the root of all our unhappiness and suffering, we can understand that those who observe and correct the identity in themselves are able to improve their state of being to an enormous degree. They will see the chaos of the identities, they will recognise the wrong identities and know how their life is ruled by them. In their quest to inculcate the true identity, they will not hide what they see is wrong, nor will they ignore major illusions. They will know where they are and what can be achieved.

The Extent of Identification

A king will have the joy or intoxication of being a king, provided he remembers that he is a king. If he came under the illusion that he was a beggar, he would have the worries and fears of a beggar. The truth may be that he continues to be the king and in everyone else's vision, he is the king, but for himself he won't have that joy or intoxication of being a king. Each time he receives a few pence, he will be happy. If he loses a pound, he will be left depressed. Similarly, when the beautiful 'Real I' is in the identity of 'I' it will experience the highest emotions possible. The emotions of peace, joy, and love are its innate, natural state. But, when it is in any identity of 'i' it will have the worries and desires related to that particular 'i'. Thus, if a person feels upset when the body or appearance is criticised, it is because during those moments, the 'Real I' considers itself to be the body, and in the identity of the body (i), praise or criticism of the body matters. (See Figure 8.)

When in an 'i' identity - praise of a pair of shoes will make the wearer happy, criticism of a man's wife will upset him, whilst victory of his country's football team will elate him. He himself may not practise his religion, but he could easily go to war against those who criticise it! In time, the empire of 'i's increases; he may identify with the organisations or activities with which he is associated. He starts identifying with some ideas, some opinions and with certain images of himself - 'I am generous,' 'I am clever,' or 'I am the one who should be given regard,' and so even more 'i's are born. Many of these are subtle images and may not be easily recognised. When we observe the variety and extent of our 'i's in a day, it will be noticed that these subtle identifications are very common and often very dominant. The expression 'body consciousness' is sometimes used to represent the false 'i' identities.

'Real I' - in True Identity

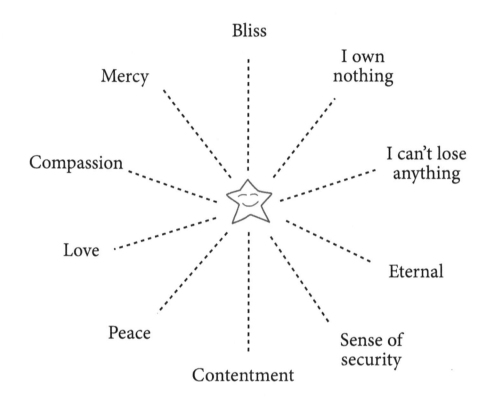

Figure 8

The birth of every 'i' means migration away from peace. Since there are many 'i's in every individual, there are many desires - some latent and others active, and therefore many reasons for discontentment or unhappiness. (See Figure 9.)

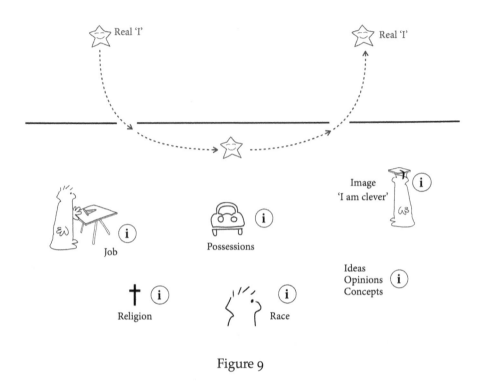

Figure 9

Consequences of Identification

When we lose the awareness of our true identity, and consider our-selves to be what we are not, we lose the grace of the original expe-rience.

A sense of security and peace is our original experience while in the identity 'I'. When one is operating from some false identity 'i', there is an instant feeling of insecurity because by definition the object of identification is transitory and so can be lost. A desire or desperation to experience security appears – and it is this despera-tion which leads to human suffering. When one is operating from 'I' identity, desire takes the form of good wishes, as it is based on security and compassion; it is a desire to give. It is different from the desire that emerges from 'i' which wishes to receive security, and so until this desire is fulfilled, the 'Real I' experiences uncertainty which manifests itself as stress, tension, worry or fear. (See Figure 10.)

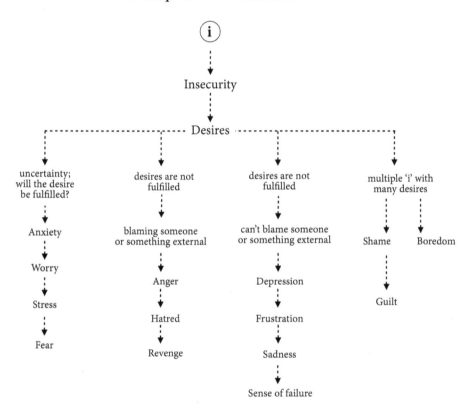

Figure 10

If the desire remains unfulfilled, the reaction will be different. If the 'blame' is placed on others, it will be in the form of anger, or its variations, such as irritability, hate or revenge. If the 'blame' is placed on the self, then the result will be depression, sadness, frustration, etc. In addition, if another person receives the object of unfulfilled desire, the result would be envy.

Since we have many 'i's, they are often in conflict with each other; as if there are many candidates, all wanting to rule. Guilt and bore-dom are the consequence of the conflict of competing 'i's. One 'i' carries out an action and another 'i' feels guilty about it, or one 'i' may undertake a task, but when another 'i' takes over in between, it feels bored with what is going on!

The Five Vices

The birth of 'i' means the birth of arrogance or impure ego state, sometimes just called 'ego'.

The desires which arise from some 'i's are very material and take the form of greed e.g. greed for more wealth from 'i' as a rich man. As the 'i' grows, insecurity also grows and so greed continues even if he achieves ten times his original need.

The desires which arise from some 'i's take the form of emotional need of other human beings or possessions which is described as 'attachment', e.g. the 'i' as a mother feels secure in the presence of her child and even if the child would be better off elsewhere, she would still prefer the child to be with her. Sometimes we can fool ourselves in thinking it is love. The word attachment is used in the context of dependency or self-centred emotional need, distinct from the experience of love.

The entire department of sex lust arises from the identity connected with lust. It is amazing that the entire lustful behaviour arises from just one of the 'i's. It may be one of the dominating 'i's that explains why so many of the theories of psychology are based on the under-standing that sex desire dominates the human race.

An 'i' which cannot be satisfied gives rise to anger, either inwardly or outwardly directed.

So, the five major manifestations of human ignorance, the five vices of arrogance, greed, attachment, lust and anger - arise from false identification.

Smriti and the Kingdom

Imagine a kingdom where there is the king, a minister and the kingdom. The role of the minister is to make the king happy. There are many candidates for the post of minister, each with different policies. Most of the candidates are not trained for the position of minister and their interests are narrow, such as war or entertainment. So, when one of these candidates comes into power, he may use the whole country, its resources and talent, for the purposes of war. Another one may use everything for the purpose of gambling, and so on.

In the kingdom, there is no fixed duration to the ministerial post. There may be changes many times during the course of one day. The strongest pushes the current incumbent out of power, until, in turn, some other candidate takes over. With each different minister, the policies change and so the priorities, motives and action change. The king enjoys himself, or suffers, based upon the policies of the changing ministers.

There is an identical model of such a kingdom within all of us, with the 'Real I' as the king - the experiencer. The identity acts as Minister, whose task is to keep the king, or the 'Real I' constantly happy. The identity can use the mind, body, wealth and time of the kingdom, and consequently the attitudes, thoughts, emotions, actions and vision are all determined by the ruling identity. There are many 'i's and one 'I' competing to gain power. When the 'i' based on lust is in the role of identity, the mind, body, wealth and time are used towards lust.

When the identity changes to that of 'i' a rich man, the priorities will change and the mind, body, time and wealth will be used accordingly. The attitudes, thoughts, vision and actions would be towards earning wealth. It is almost as though a different person is now in the same body.

Given that there are numerous 'i's and only one 'I' - there are many incompetent candidates for minister, and only one competent candidate. Until the identity of 'I' becomes the constant ruler, the mind, body and wealth will be constantly diverted from one direction to another under the changing role of the many incompetent 'i' identities.

The Human Psyche

If it were possible to take a photograph of the human psyche showing the various identities which a person passes through during the day, we would have a picture similar to the one below. (See Figure 11.)

There are many false identities that dominate our psyche. We are continually moving from one false identity (i) to another. Some of these 'i's are stronger than others. Different people have different dominating identities - some may identify strongly with their profession, others with their religion or family, but we all have most of the usual identifications.

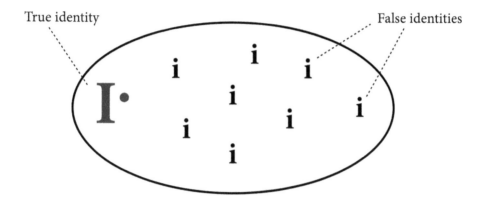

Figure 11

The reason why some of our 'i's dominate, is because we have spent more time in these particular identities. In addition, each and every second we experience pleasure or joy from a particular identity, that becomes nourishment for that identity and consequently it becomes more dominant. Intoxication of the ego feeds the ego. This leads us to infer that indulging in the so-called pleasures of the world - pleasures from 'i' identities (arrogance, greed, lust, attachment, and so on), tends to feed our identifications. Similarly, spending more time in the 'I' identity, or experiencing joy from the 'I' identity helps to move us towards the dominance of the 'I' identity.

Chapter 4

VINASH FORCES

We mentioned earlier that there are laws in nature which seek stability - and therefore, various forces are generated to redress the balance if things deviate away from the stable state. For example, when a person lifts a stone, he also generates the forces which eventually bring that stone back to ground level. The stone may be used in a building, and may stay there for 100 years, but that force to bring it to the ground will continue to act until one day the stone falls down. Nature has patience. We can also take the example of a man stretching a spring. The more he stretches it, he generates forces to bring it back to its original stable state.

Now, let us consider the human psyche. If the reality of a human being is that he is a soul, his function of identity must also be of 'I' constantly and naturally. However, if for any reason, he stretches his identity away from 'I' to a false identity 'i', (as in Figure 12) in that process he will give birth to forces that are meant to destroy the 'i's from the psyche so that the original stable state is achieved. These forces we will call Vinash forces.

These Vinash forces are not physical forces, but present themselves as unpleasant circumstances or misfortunes, since only unpleasant

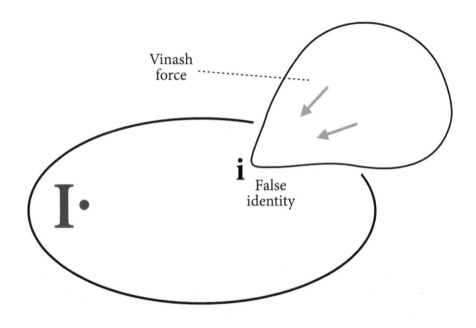

Figure 12

circumstances or pain can force us to remove 'i's. They are specifically tailor made for the 'i's which a person possesses. We create 'i's based on the body, relationships, external circumstances such as job, status, and so on, and in more subtle ways based on environment and senses. In consequence, the Vinash forces of some 'i's present themselves through the body, some through relationships, some through circumstance and some through environment. All misfortunes experienced by an individual is a Vinash force in action.

Vinash forces of different 'i's act or close down at different times and it is quite possible for a person with many false identities ('i's) to lead an apparently comfortable life for some time. Nevertheless the build-up of Vinash force continues and unless something is done about these abnormal 'i's in the psyche, sooner or later the Vinash forces will invade the life of that person. Thus, his so-called life circumstances - his health, his social and financial circumstances, how he is treated by others and by matter - every detail is a reaction to the false identity that he carries. False identities will even inspire certain behaviours from others. If we realise this phenomenon, it tells us that the outside world of matter and our circumstances are created totally by our own psyche. (See Figure 13.)

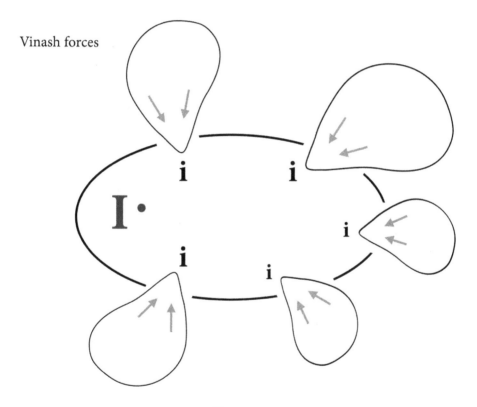

Figure 13

We can observe this phenomenon of Vinash forces in our day to day life. As mentioned earlier 'i' identity is essentially a false ego. If, within a certain gathering, one person exhibits overt arrogance based on his status or possessions, we can notice that immediately the others in the gathering will react to his arrogance and can even be inspired to oppose him, or to knock him down, even though he did not harm them. The presence of arrogance was sufficient to invite opposition. The same phenomenon operates at a more subtle level through circumstances and matter.

The more a person feeds the false 'i's, the more he invites unpleasant circumstances into his life to destroy them. As he observes the false 'i's and drops them, and as he nurtures the identity of 'I' within his psyche, he invites positive situations towards himself - and a world with pleasant circumstances presents itself. The world that matches the constant identity of 'I' is a world completely without Vinash force. He will find himself being lucky in life.

Our natural and original experience of this physical world is beautiful and harmonious and can be likened to a beautiful painting. Originally, when our identity was of 'I' - the world and the life that was presented to us was perfect and full of harmony, beauty, peace and joy. As we gave birth to the identity of 'i's and fed them, we gave birth to the Vinash forces like patches of dirt on the painting, until our whole life and circumstances became a series of different forms of Vinash forces acting in succession. It is as if the original painting has become completely covered with patches of dirt. However, if these abnormal identities are removed through knowledge and understanding, then the Vinash forces are also nullified automatically. Those who experiment with this, bring about a major change in their own world. It becomes a world of harmony, peace, joy and love. If such a change in the human psyche takes place collectively, the whole of society, land and climate - the world - has to change to match this psychic change. Conversely, if the collective growth of 'i's continues unabated, then the Vinash forces will also escalate and ultimately invade human civilization in the form of collective destruction. In the name of progress, achievement, freedom and the pursuit of pleasure, global ego-consciousness has exploded over the past 80 years. There are large and growing stockpiles of Vinash forces in the world.

Physical Illness

Whenever a Vinash force acts, it does so to eradicate a particular 'i' and so is tailor-made for that 'i'. For instance, if the 'i' is associated with a physical object then the Vinash force will manifest as the loss or damage of that object. If the 'i' is in association with a role, e.g. a professor, then the Vinash force may take the form of the loss of that job. Thus, every Vinash force is specific to each particular 'i'. For example, there was a girl, Laura, who was a performer on the stage and used to being admired for her beauty and popularity. One day Laura and her friends had a car accident and Laura sustained head injury and she became temporarily unconscious. When she came round, she asked her friends to give her a mirror to see herself. When she saw her swollen face, full of cuts and bruises, in her words, she couldn't stop crying for hours. The reason for her pain was not the physical pain, but the horror of seeing her physical appearance in that state in the mirror. During this time, she realised how big an ego she had created based on her pretty face. She also realised that this situation had drawn her attention to something she had not observed herself… the ego based on appearance. This concept of Vinash force tells us that we invite situations towards us from our own psyche. The expression 'pride comes before the fall' is true except that pride is the cause of the fall.

We have explained that the 'i's are first born and then fed during moments of corresponding intoxication. We cannot experience pleasure or intoxication unless we are in the corresponding identity. Pleasure through the senses is typically one of our major sources of physical pleasures. Because this is not experienced in the identity of 'I', it can only feed identities of 'i's. These sense-related 'i's are more subtle and less easily observed than other 'i's. Since they are created through the senses (that is through the body), any Vinash forces towards them will also act through the body and will manifest through disharmony in the body systems - as one or another form of physical illness. This is the foundation for all human illness. Henceforth, we shall refer to the identity of 'i's related to the senses as S'i's.

The human body has senses for the purpose of providing information from the external world to the Real 'I'. When one is in the identity of 'I' there is the highest inner joy and the senses are used for what they were originally intended, that is, to provide information. When the Real 'I' loses its True identity it does drift into the identities of S'i's when in contact with objects of the senses.

Since we have five senses; vision, hearing, touch, smell and taste, there are five main varieties of S'i's. When one is in the identity of 'S'i' Vision, his desires, thoughts and actions will revolve around pleasure through the eyes, e.g. colours, paintings, TV, human appearances, and so on. When one is in the identity of S'i' Touch, his desires, thoughts and actions will revolve around physical touch or sex, and so on. Interaction then will definitely feed the bandit (S'i') hiding inside.

When we start feeding these S'i's by taking pleasure through any of these senses and the S'i's grow, they build up proportionate Vinash forces. Sooner or later, these Vinash forces start to invade our life. The Vinash forces associated with the different S'i's present themselves differently: the Vinash force to S'i' Touch may present itself as chronic arthritis, while the Vinash force to S'i' Vision may present itself as Hyperthyroidism .

Within each of these five main varieties, there would be sub-classification based on various modalities of sensations. Thus, within S'i' Taste, one may have many sub-types related to various different tastes, and thus their Vinash force would also be different to each other. The combined Vinash forces of more than one S 'i' would present themselves as a major illness. Thus the aetiology of various illnesses could reside in the permutation and combination of the Vinash forces of various S'i's. In time, people go for more and more sensual stimulation and for grosser modalities of pleasures through the body. Stimulation of the body and senses is also done through smoking, drugs, alcohol, movements, etc. It has to be emphasised that the process of feeding the S'i's is not the mere use of the sense organs; S'i's only grow when the sense organs are used for indulgence.

If we want to ensure that we are no longer feeding the S'i's, then every time we are about to come in contact with a sense object, for instance, before a meal, we need to reinforce the 'I' identity and experience the joy from that identity, otherwise, we would eat the same meal from an 'i' identity. This is also the most effective way of eradicating the S'i's from the psyche and thus a true cure for physical illness - both for the present and for the future. It is as if nature tells us that we have a right to experience super-sensual pleasures, and that sense pleasures are illegitimate.

It is not necessary to go into detail over the different types of S'i's and their exact relationship with different illnesses because firstly, the remedy is the same for all, and secondly, everyone gives birth to almost every variety of S'i's - the difference is just in their relative intensity and dominance. If one would like to pursue this further and know the exact relationship between S'i's and illness, there are certain clues. The different sense organs reach the soul through different modes:-

· Touch and hearing reach the soul through mechanical movements or mechanical pressure e.g. touch receptors, Tympanic membrane, and inner ear hair cells.

· Taste and smell reach the soul through chemical reactions within the taste buds or olfactory receptors.

· Sight reaches the soul through metabolic changes in response to heat and light within the retinal cells.

In other words, the soul experiences pleasures in response to mechanical pressure, chemical reaction or metabolic changes within the body. Thus the Vinash forces that emerge due to these specific S'i's are more likely to be of a similar mode:

S'i' touch is more likely to affect the systems where there are movements, e.g. gastro-intestinal tract, striated muscles, joints or various abnormalities in developmental movements

S'i' hearing, from our experience, affects the other movements but also the nervous system - possibly movement of the action potential down the nerve fibre or across various synapses.

S'i' taste and S'i' smell are more likely to affect the biochemical processes; e.g. endocrines, digestive juices, and so on.

S'i' vision tends to affect the organs that deal with metabolism, e.g. liver, thyroid, etc., and also the metabolic processes.

Chapter 5

THE SECOND OPTION

The Alloy in the identity

By now, we must be aware of the seriousness of having the wrong identity. Imagine a person, who believed deep inside that he was a donkey. He then would act like a donkey, carry the worries of a donkey, and suffer because of the problems of a donkey, e.g. having less hay. One of the important milestones in our progress is to realise very clearly our present situation. We are not very different from the person in the example. Here, the eternal and beautiful beings of light are deeply convinced that they are the bodies. They have the worries about the body and they suffer because of the problems of the body. When they are told that they are truly beings of light, it appears to be a strange idea and they may not realise what they have ignored. This state of illusion is the identity of 'i'.

Identification with the body is a very deep identity because many many years are spent in that identification. Also, because the whole of society is in the same boat, it reinforces the wrong identity. When everyone commits the same crime, it ceases to be viewed as a crime.

Even if one knows that the herd is moving towards a slaughter house, it still requires courage to move away from the herd.

For the soul to be free from the identities of 'i's, means to be aware of itself as an eternal, free, non-physical being, naturally. In that awareness, one experiences peace, joy and compassion regardless of the changing physical world. It is a state in which one doesn't worry and behave as everyone else does around you. It is different to just having the knowledge of soul. In fact, knowledge by itself doesn't remove the identities of 'i's at all. These various identities of 'i's are like an alloy within gold, as opposed to the dust on the surface, and so the treatment to separate them has got to be precise. To separate an alloy from gold, one needs to melt the metal. One mechanism that can rid the soul of the identities of 'i's is severe pain or the Vinash forces. Extreme suffering or destruction is the sort of treatment that can eventually treat the soul.

However, as we mentioned in Chapter I, we humans learn by one of the two ways - either through pain or through wisdom. The subsequent discussion explores the second of these two options. We shall reach our objective from many angles and an attempt is made to discuss some of the important practices. The student will realise the value of these practices only after their application and see the changes and practical benefits. Putting into practice any one of the methods makes the practice of the others easier and they complement each other, and so one may place more emphasis on one or the other, depending on what suits him the best at that particular time.

The Objective

Figure 14 (A) shows the present state of a person's psyche. There is a dominance of 'i' identities, with 'I' identity reduced to insignificance, and on top of that, certain 'i' identities are shown growing larger. Diagram (B) shows our original identity of 'I', which is our potential. (See Figure 14.)

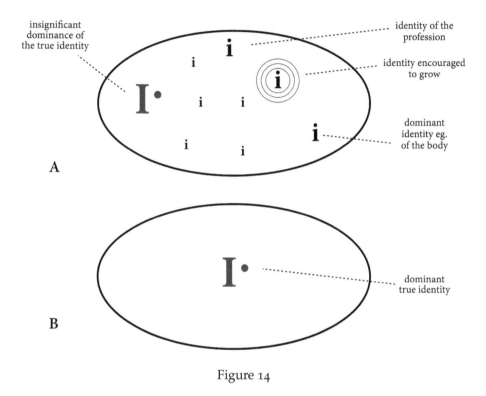

Figure 14

Our objective is to achieve our full potential and the key formula used here is to spend more and more time in the identity of 'I', to experience peace and bliss while in the identity of 'I', and to resist the unconscious drift into 'i's or to resist any type of pleasures which feed 'i's.

As we spend more and more time in the identity of 'I' and experience happiness from there, the dominance of 'I' identity will increase, and it will become more and more natural to stay in that identity. As the light increases, the darkness disappears automatically - we do not need to make separate effort to remove darkness. In the same way as identity of 'I' increases, the dominance of identity of 'i's becomes less and less, and finally, just with this persistence, we shall achieve total identity of 'I' as shown in diagram (B). The subsequent discussion is aimed towards understanding the different approaches towards this same objective.

Soul and the Body

If we study the identities of the population, in this age, we will find that the most dominant identity (i) is in relation to the body. Each one thinks of himself or herself based on the body; shape, gender, appearance, posture, and so on. In other words, one of the strongest competition for the 'I' smriti is the smriti based on the body.

Just as we use the words in first person, second person and third person in speech, in the same way, in our attitude and perception also, we treat certain things in first, second or third person. The entities that we identify with are often treated in first person within our perception. We are less likely to identify with the same intensity anything which is the second or third person in our attitude or perception. (See Figure 15.)

For example, when a person says, 'I am sitting on the chair' the chair is seen in third person and so he won't identify with the chair. However, we see that he is already identifying with the body because truly the body is sitting on the chair and he is using the word 'I' for the 'body' - he is using the first person tense for the body.

So, if we want to break that identification with the body, we just need to treat the body in third person (or second person). Thus, the attitude and the expressions will be:

'I am making the body sit on the chair,'
'I am making the body walk,' instead of 'I am walking,' or
'I am feeding the body,' instead of 'I am eating.'

'Real I'

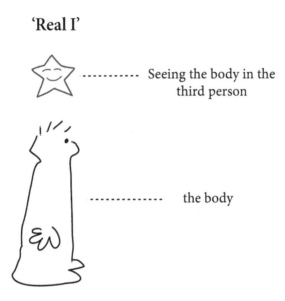

Seeing the body in the
third person

the body

Figure 15

With this practice, one finds oneself in the identity of a bodiless being using the body. We can have this attitude during almost every
activity. For example, someone can say to himself 'This body is
resting here. I now make the body rise up. I am turning it round; I
am making it walk' and so on. It is as if one stands behind the body
and sees the body in third person.

Introspection - Self Observation

We mentioned earlier that identity is a continuous function taking
place in us. It is a subtle function, so people normally do not notice
the identity that rules them, nor do they bother to know about how
often the identity changes in them over a period of time. One very
useful practice for us, is to observe this function within us and to see

the identity at different times. How often are we aware of ourselves as non-physical and secure beings of light? Observing our own identity can be a beautiful game that we can play with ourselves.

We know from experience that suffering of any kind increases our potential to learn. Attempting to observe our identity during those moments can be very rewarding. We also know that suffering exists only when we are in the 'i' identity. In the identity of 'I', we are immune to any form of suffering, under any provocation. So during the moments when we experience anxiety, annoyance, frustration, or when we feel criticised or unsuccessful, there is a rule of the 'i' identity, and we need to recognise those 'i's.

Whenever we spot the 'i' identity, we automatically see the contrast and are reminded of the 'I' identity and our security. We are then able to see the 'i' in third person, from a platform of peace and security of 'I'. During those moments, the destruction of 'i' is not seen as our destruction. Within seconds, we can experience freedom from anxiety, anger, or frustration. Thus, observation of 'i' is rather significant, and accurate observation means half the battle is won. When we are in the identity of 'I', all the hostile, external events can at most scratch the 'i's or destroy the burden of 'i's, but soul remains happy about that, and the attitude of the soul will be 'what I am, I remain!'; 'I cannot be deprived; I can only be freed'.

We should be aware that when the circumstances around us provide comfort, pleasure, praise to 'i's, i.e. small desires get fulfilled, this does create a false sense of security, and it is possible for 'i's to escape self-observation.

Self - Remembering

Each and every second we spend in any one identity ('i'), that particular identity is fed and it grows. Each and every second we experience happiness because one of the 'i's is fed, that particular 'i' grows and becomes dominant. For this reason, in Figure 14, the 'i's are shown in different sizes, representing different degrees of dominance.

The predominant identities in one person will be different from those in another, e.g. one person will identify strongly with his job, while another with his religion and he would be less concerned about the arrogance due to his job. The reasons why some identities are more dominant than others are that either more time has been spent in those identities, or the person has experienced some degree of pleasure being in a particular identity.

Praise, success, glory of objects around a person, or of his roles, can act as a strong temptation to identify with those objects or roles, and thus experience pleasure from them. The more he experiences pleasure through a certain identity, the more dominant that identity becomes, and the more often it will rule the psyche. It has to be clarified that success and glory by itself cannot be wrong but when that becomes the basis of one's pleasure, only then we feed a wrong identity.

It is possible for us to naturally and constantly be aware of ourselves as eternal, peaceful, conscious beings of light, experiencing inner joy, contentment and love. It is also possible to be associated with the various entities and roles without identifying with them. If we wish to enjoy this state, then the dominance of the identity of 'I' must be raised from its present negligible representation in the psyche to a level where we are naturally in the identity of 'I'. To bring about such a reversal of the identity in the psyche, we have to apply the same process that caused the 'i's to dominate in the first place. We just need to spend more and more time in the conscious awareness of the soul - that is, in the identity of 'I'. We need to collect seconds and minutes. Each and every second spent in the awareness of I feeds the identity I and helps it grow - helps it to become more dominant. This exercise can be called Self-Remembering or Soul Consciousness. (See Figure 16.)

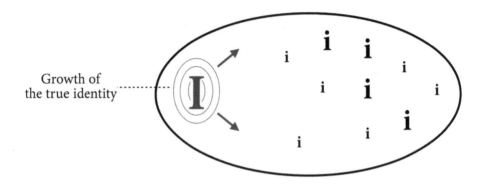

Figure 16

Being a Guest

We will note that when one feels that he owns any objects, body or individuals, there are greater chances of identification with them in time. In a situation where there is no sense of 'my' or 'mine', identification is also less likely; e.g. if I am a guest in someone's house, there may be very beautiful objects and lots of praise is showered on those objects from all around, but its not likely that I will be affected by that praise. Similarly, if there is any criticism of the objects I will not feel that 'I' am being criticised - I will be free! I didn't use those famous pronouns 'my, mine'! As a guest, I enjoyed the peace and joy of being a guest, which is very different to the intoxication that the host experiences on hearing the praise. The peace and joy of the guest is constant and pure; free from the anxiety of criticism or failure.

Now, let us see the role of the eternal soul on the earth. This eternal 'being', soul, takes the body, uses the house, car, dress, and so on, during his lifetime - which is a short period. When the moment of death arrives it leaves everything behind. In other words, the soul plays a temporary part or pays a short visit to the earth, like a guest. This is our true relationship to the planet. We are guests on this planet.

We saw earlier that we don't own anything, and our expression should be 'everything that I use is not "mine" even the body I use is not mine'; 'I am a guest in this body and in this world'. 'Further, what "I" truly have, no-one can take away from me'. 'As a guest, I use many things, but while using them I am aware that I might have to leave them behind any time'. With this attitude of the 'guest', there is automatically freedom from possessiveness and identification. We find ourselves in the identity of 'I'.

So whilst we consider ourselves to be 'guests' on earth, we will experience these pure emotions and when we act, our actions will be motivated by compassion and joy. As 'guests' we will experience freedom and peace, but we won't be careless. Pure compassion won't allow us to be careless. We might be in association with many precious things, we might be using and looking after many things, but we will always be aware that nothing belongs to us - we are just 'Trustees' of all these possessions. We will use them for the maximum benefit of most - out of compassion. To live with compassion will be our greatest joy. Even close relations or children won't be seen with possession using the word 'mine', but rather we are 'Trustees' who have a duty to look after them. No-one owns anyone.

The Observer

The attitude of seeing the body in third person and without a sense of possession is essential in any practice of soul consciousness. We mentioned earlier about the practice of seeing oneself as a guest in the body. In that, one very naturally treats the body in third person, because soul is the guest in the body. We can take it a step further. Just as a guest may be in a certain house, looking out through the windows of the house at the town outside, in the same way, we can see the body as a house, and the eyes as the windows of that house. The expressions will be 'The soul who is a guest, is looking out through the windows of this body. "I" am sitting just behind these windows. "I" am observing the world outside, including the body, through these windows'. With this practice, we can naturally create and maintain the identity of 'I'.

'The Actor' and 'The Role'

So far, we have seen how we identify with physical objects. We know that we also identify with the various roles that we play. Whatever the soul was before it entered the body, it remains the same, even whilst using the body. However, once in the body, the soul comes into its different roles through the body, e.g. son, daughter, wife, doctor, lawyer, president of some club, and so on, and in time, it starts identifying with some of those roles which it plays.

As we identify ourselves with our roles, in time we find it painful to give them up, e.g. if someone has been playing the role of a President over a period of years and then has to give up that role, he might find it painful. Over the years he has been nurturing an 'i' of being a President and now feels that 'i' is being destroyed. Similarly, someone who identifies strongly as a mother and then loses her child will suffer greatly because 'i' as a mother is also made to 'die' and that death is painful.

If we live in truth about ourselves, in the identity of 'I', then there wouldn't be any suffering. We will see the different roles such as lawyer, husband, president and so on, in the third person. We will see it as a drama, where an actor plays different roles and puts on different masks but all the time remains aware as to who he is, i.e. who he is behind the masks and the different roles. An actor may be playing the role of a king who experiences victory or defeat in the drama, but the actor himself knows that this is not his victory or his defeat for he knows that he is Mr Smith and is therefore beyond the circumstances in which the character finds himself in the drama.

We are eternal beings playing different temporary roles. Whilst playing these different temporary roles, we just need to remind ourselves that we are 'actors'. Behind the roles that we play, we are souls. Different actors have different roles - some have the role of a hero, some have the role of a villain. We won't judge the other person by the role that he is playing and we won't forget ourselves as to who we are behind the roles.

During a play, whilst an actor is playing his role, he also observes the drama going on around him, and he appreciates the different scenes in the drama. He is also the observer of the drama. In fact, any actor always happens to be an observer of the drama including the character he is playing. We all have experienced at some stage being the observers of a drama. When we are observers we experience a special peace and joy which is a state of peace from non-identification. If we don't identify with the roles or events in the drama we will enjoy it regardless of the character or role we are playing - who wins, who dies, or whatever takes place.

We will remain curious to see the events and will enjoy them as they unfold . However, should we start to identify with any character in the drama, especially the character we are playing; we would stop being the detached observers. That state can best be described as severe confusion and then our happiness would be dependent on the fortune of that character. We would become anxious to see what will happen to that character, and we would stop enjoying the drama from a state of equanimity. We might become angry or upset over certain events or over the end result, or we could find ourselves opposing certain events. Identification leads to desires and so we begin to impose conditions on the events of the drama.

We are eternally observers in this unlimited world drama. This earth has to be looked upon as a stage and the various events which take place have to be observed without identifying with the various characters of the drama, the roles that we play or with the events themselves. If we become the observers even for a few minutes, during those minutes we will automatically be in 'I' identity. Eventually, when we act, we will act from the identity of 'I' and we will see our roles in third person, and as we act out our roles, there will be a state of peace.

Different Approaches towards Self-Remembering

We have to experience ourselves repeatedly as what we truly are; eternal, peaceful, loving beings, subtle light; we are infinitesimally small stars of conscious light with purity, peace and bliss; this is accurate self-remembering, but at different times different practices help create this stage. The following analogies might help in this practice.

· To see myself as a guest in this body and so a guest in this world

· To see myself as a trustee; for example in a situation with children or possessions

· To remind myself that I am an actor playing this particular role

· To be a detached observer of the drama

· To see myself as a traveller passing through this life - a traveller in time

· To consider myself as the driver of this body

· To look out at the world outside through the windows of the body, i.e. the eyes

· To see myself as an incarnate in the body, one who uses the body for a certain noble purpose

In order to increase the amount of time we spend in self-remembering and resist the unconscious drift into identification, we may have to use different approaches appropriate to the situations and the time.

A meditation experience
www.cambridgeinnerspace.org/med-2

Chapter 6

REMEMBRANCE

The Vision

There is a story that a flower was shown to four different individuals. The artist amongst them saw the beauty of the flower, the perfection of colours and the symmetry. The botanist saw that it had eight stamens, and that its calyx was unusually coloured. The herbalist saw the medicinal value of the petals, and the businessman saw the present price of that flower in the market. The example summarises how our vision is influenced by our identity. Our vision of other people is similarly influenced by our identity. (See Figure 17.)

In the above diagram the human psyche is shown containing some of the possible identities. When someone identifies himself with his profession, it is as if he is standing on the platform of 'i' (Professor), and from this platform he will see others by their profession: if he identifies with his car, e.g. 'i' (Porsche), he will see others by the type of car they drive: if he identifies with his religion, 'i' (Christian), he will see others by their religion; if he identifies with his physical body or appearance then others will be seen for their bodies. He will see the various external layers in another and his vision will stop there.

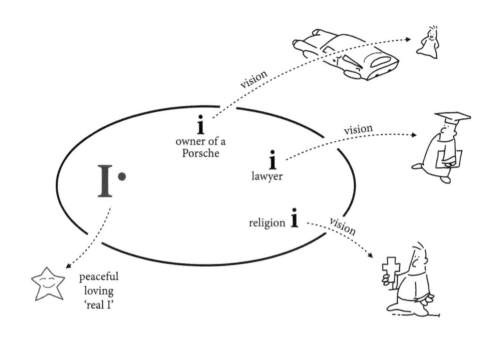

Figure 17

However, if he stands on the platform of his 'I' identity, he would see something very different in others. He would see peaceful and loving souls. He would ignore the various external covers and even their present behaviour, which could be due to identification and he would see others by their original nature, as peaceful, loving beings like himself: as his brothers. This vision would be his vision naturally if he himself has an 'I' identity.

Since at the present moment we are starting with a very rudimentary 'I' identity, our vision won't be the highest, naturally. In fact, our aim at the moment is to find a method to increase those moments spent in 'I' identity, especially whilst we are in the company of others. We can achieve this by paying attention to our vision. Whilst in the company of others, we can make a deliberate practice of seeing the soul in others - to see them as peaceful beings of light, behind those particular bodies. With such a vision, there will be respect and brotherly love for others, but even more important, we ourselves will be brought into the 'I' identity. Therefore, this is an indirect but a very precious method towards self-progress. Since vision and thoughts are easier to control than identity we just need to be attentive to what we see and think of others, and if we can see them as souls, our thoughts will remain subtle enough to create soul consciousness, i.e. 'I' identity in us.

The Third Eye

We discussed in Chapter II, the existence of the unmanifest world. We also know that we give disproportionate importance to the manifest world in comparison to the unmanifest world in our minds and attitudes. The practice of seeing others as non-physical beings and seeing the physical body as the temporary instrument used by the soul is a new vision and new attitude for most of us. The physical eyes cannot see these aspects, but we can see the soul with its qualities, with the 'eye of the mind '. We do use the 'eye of the mind' in our ordinary life any way. In that sense, it is not an unknown function. For instance, if you meet a person for the first time, you may see the physical body, and carry a certain image of that person. But if you happen to meet him again the next day and by then know his various qualities, habits, past actions, likes, etc., your vision will be different. The physical eyes will still see the body, but the eye of the mind will see his past, his qualities, etc.

When one uses the 'eye of the mind' with knowledge, i.e. when one is able to see others and the world around in total clarity, in truth, then it is called using the third eye. Thus, seeing the soul with its original qualities of peace, love and compassion, is the vision through the third eye. It is different from the gross vision of the role or characters that were seen in the past.

The Supreme Being

Even though our vision of others as a soul is the right vision and has its benefits, yet we cannot see it as one of our main methods towards achieving 'I' identity because there are many difficulties in the practice. When we look at another person and if we know his job, religion, country, relations, and his past actions, we won't find it easy to see him constantly as a soul; we won't be able to ignore the physical appearance of the body. Therefore, our thought will swing from seeing the soul one moment to seeing the professor or the husband, the friend or a tall thin body, the next moment. Consequently, we won't be able to locate ourselves in the identity of 'I' either, and we will also swing into different 'i's ourselves.

Here, the understanding of The Being who does not come into a body or live a life like others, is of special significance. If this Being does not come into a body like others, it means He is also free from the various associations with the body, job, race, nationality, religion, and so on. (A masculine pronoun is used for the absence of a neutral personal pronoun in English language). Because of the absence of any associations, He will be unlikely to identify with the physical world and various roles, as others do. In other words, He remains in absolute soul consciousness - totally free from any 'i' identity. (See Figure 18.)

If He is constantly soul conscious, it implies that He remains constantly in the Original state, having the original experience and qualities. He will be in the knowledge of His own eternity, his security, and thus, he will be free from desires, (described as a state of purity). The absolute security will allow the original feelings to emerge and so there will be peace, love, compassion, joy and bliss. Since this Being is constantly free from desires, He won't have any conditions or demands from anything or anyone, thus qualities

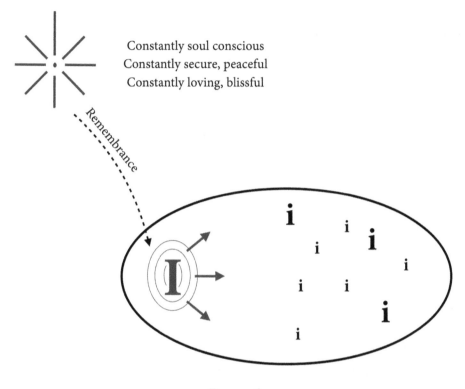

Constantly soul conscious
Constantly secure, peaceful
Constantly loving, blissful

Remembrance

Figure 18

such as love will be unconditional and unlimited. All these are the supreme qualities and so we can call this being the Supreme Being.

Earlier, when the example was given of someone trying to have a pure vision of soul towards others, difficulties arose due to the various physical attributes with which others were associated. Now, when he turns his vision towards the Supreme Being - all that he experiences are the pure qualities of the soul – peace, bliss, selfless love, contentment, absence of desires, purity, truth, wisdom and benevolence. Here is a Being with a very definite personality, a certain identity, a certain attitude and vision, but without any physical attributes. So each time a person thinks of this Being, he is prevented from drifting into any of the 'i' identities because there are no associations or attributes which can interest those false identities. Since he is observing and experiencing the pure qualities of soul when he thinks of the Supreme Being, it helps himself stay in the identity of 'I' automatically.

The experience of the Supreme Being cannot emerge, when we are in any false identity; we can think of Him accurately only when we are in the highest identity of 'I' ourselves. In that sense, it is the noblest thought. The practice to keep thoughts focussed on the Supreme Being in this way is called Yoga. This is the most precious formula for the upliftment of the human race.

Is He Our Imagination?

As our practice of 'I' identity improves, as our vision is more and more from the third eye and as our intellect is able to grasp the subtleties, we will know and realise many things which cannot be shown to us in the laboratory. In the meantime, it is quite natural for us to question 'Is the Supreme Being our imagination? or 'Does He really exist?' The subject will be much clearer as we go through the remaining chapters but at this stage, we can take the position that it does not matter!

All the time people never question when they see magazine pictures, that they are not the real people, they are just pictures. They also think of various fictitious characters from novels and films who they know do not even exist. Even though they are the fictitious characters, those thoughts certainly feed some false identities within us. All of this has left us with very bloated false identities. The kind of thoughts we have definitely nourishes the corresponding identity. The thought of the Supreme Being nourishes the 'I' identity in us. It has the immediate benefit of creating the 'I' identity, and refining our intellect. A subtle and refined intellect is necessary even to know ourselves properly. In time our understanding of the Supreme Being will improve. We will experience the facets of the Supreme Being that were not seen or experienced earlier.

Just as at a physical level, we may be introduced to a person, say a president of a certain country just by his description. Even though we didn't meet him, yet we can think of him and his qualities based on his description. We may get inspired by his qualities and may bring about certain changes in our lives. In time, we may come to meet him personally and know him better. But this meeting is not essential on the first day, and it is not a precondition to think of him.

In the same way, we can direct our mind towards the qualities, identity and feelings of the Supreme Being based on the preliminary introduction that we have of Him. Our knowledge of His beauty will continue to expand and relationship will continue to be closer.

Qualities of the Supreme Being

The qualities of the Supreme Being are the qualities of the soul in the identity of 'I'. The difference between the Supreme Being and humans is that the Supreme Being is constantly in the identity of 'I'. There is no possibility of even a trace of false identity in Him. In humans, false identities lead to insecurities, and that prevents the experience of their original qualities, just as rust can obscure the shine of a beautiful metal. Absence of any trace of insecurities enables the Supreme Being to remain beautiful constantly; the original qualities express themselves freely, in a limitless fashion,

The Supreme Being

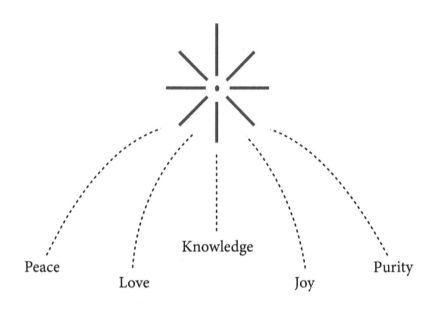

Peace

Love

Knowledge

Joy

Purity

Constantly in truth and clarity

In the identity of the 'true I'

Constantly secure

Without the sense of 'my'

Figure 19

constantly and unconditionally. That is why He can be compared to an ocean. (See Figure 19.)

At the present time, when all human beings are deeply into false identities and into insecurities, the Supreme Being stands in total contrast to everyone else. As discussed earlier, He has the highest knowledge – truth about Himself and about human beings. We also saw that in the identity of 'I', He knows His eternity and experiences a deep sense of security. Because of this sense of security the Supreme Being is free from any desires, expectations, demands and conditions. He remains in peace. It is a state of constant inner peace. No external situation can disturb this peace.

Other feelings that emerge in the environment of security are love and compassion. The one who loves, experiences his own love. In that sense, we can only experience our own love. We all know how pleasant the emotion of love is! Given the choice, everyone would like to stay in a state of love constantly. But human insecurities, un-fulfilled expectations, demands or desires blocks this delicate and precious emotion and it is allowed to express itself only when the desires are fulfilled - conditional love. At other times, humans opt for some transitory insignificant material gains in preference to the feeling of inner love and compassion. The Supreme Being loves constantly. He loves in the face of disrespect. He loves to love. His love is unconditional, which means it continues regardless of harm, loss, criticism, disobedience, inefficiency, efficiency, and so on. His love expresses itself as benevolence. Another feeling that expresses itself in the atmosphere of security is bliss. Again, with human beings, happiness is conditional, depending on external cir-cumstances, on the fulfilment of desires. With the Supreme Being, bliss is a natural state, bliss from detachment, an inner state, free from the anxiety of losing it. Thus, the Supreme Being is unique in that He owns nothing and is incorporeal, yet He is the ocean of knowledge, purity, peace, love, and bliss.

Vision of the Supreme Being

We discussed earlier about our vision of other people. We are also very sensitive in picking up the vision others have towards us. The moment we meet someone, consciously or unconsciously, we try to recognise the vision that person has of us. It may be one of high respect or one based on our defects.

Since the attitude or the way others speak to us is based on their vision of us, we can be fairly accurate in registering exactly what others see in us. It doesn't stop there. The vision of others can also promote a certain identity in us. Thus, when we are in the company of relatives, our identity is more likely to be in the corresponding roles, e.g. husband or father, and this is largely because of their vision. It is as if others can pin us into certain identities if we are careless. This happens, even if we just think of others. It is as if during those moments, we also think of their vision of us and the identity comes accordingly.

Now, let us see the vision of the Supreme Being. It was said earlier that our own vision of others is based on our identity. If we are in the identity of our job, then our vision of others will be based on their jobs. When we are in the identity of 'I ' we will see beautiful and eternal soul in others. Since the Supreme Being is constantly in the identity of 'I', His vision of others is constantly the highest. He is constantly aware of our highest destiny and sees the highest in us all the time. Regardless of what we think of ourselves or our present actions and behaviour - He sees an Angel within us. This is because the soul is a being who is secure, peaceful, blissful, compassionate towards all, constantly loving and content. We can afford to use the word 'angel' here - those qualities are used to describe an angel. A soul in the identity of 'I' is an Angel.

So each time our thoughts are directed towards the Supreme Being, we must also be aware of His vision of us. This vision creates within us the highest identity - that of an angel - identity of 'I'. No one else in this world would naturally have this vision towards others and so if we have a choice to think about others or the Supreme Being - we should realise the great difference in the net result caused by these two different thoughts.

Relationships with the Supreme Being

So far, we have been introduced to the Supreme Being with some of his qualities. By now we also know His personality. This is sufficient information for us to think of Him, to admire Him and to love Him. Take an example where a person is introduced to a king. To start with, it may remain a distant relationship. He may occasionally think of the king. In time, as he may come to know his various qualities, say, courage or wisdom, he may take inspiration from him and admire him. Later if the opportunity arises, they may become friends and in time, they may become a close companions.

Our relationship with the Supreme Being takes on a similar pattern. There was a time when we didn't know Him, and we didn't know His qualities. When we are introduced to Him for the first time, there may be difficulty to stabilise our minds on Him. Later, we find it easier to see Him as our friend, and to experience His presence. As the recognition of the Supreme Being improves, we find it a privilege to be in His company, to think of Him; and to experience His friendship. Since He is the one who loves unconditionally, He is only too pleased to be our friend. Then, how close a relationship we would like to take all depends on us. We can experience Him as our closest companion, a very close friend, or a master (guide). We can stay in the excitement of having such a perfect and highest being as our close friend.

The Total Experience

We have seen that the various 'i's become dominant in our identity because we experience a certain pleasure or happiness from them. The same process applies to the identity of 'I'. If our aim is to promote the identity of 'I' then to start with we need to stay in this identity, but even more important, will be to experience happiness in this identity. When we think of the Supreme Being with all his qualities, as a very personal Being, we come to love Him, and love is the highest form of happiness. Further still, we can see the Supreme Being in our various relationships, e.g. like our friend, one with whom we can place our trust and share our secrets. We can experience the Supreme Being as our Father - one who inspires and encourages, one who shows us perfect qualities. We can also experience the qualities of our Mother - one who cleans, protects, forgives, supports, etc.

Thus, seeing the Supreme Being with His original beautiful personality, and knowing His close relationship to us, adds to a deep feeling of love. The entire relationship is very stable without any insecurities or anxieties (unlike other relationships) because the relationship is eternal. This experience of peace, love and bliss, without any anxiety or insecurity is like a total experience. It is this experience that purifies our psyche of false identities.

The Supreme Region

So far, we have seen how the company of other human beings, or the thoughts of others influences our identity. We have also seen how the thought of the Supreme Being takes us into the highest identity. If we go further we will see that we are also influenced by matter and material objects, places and towns. If we are sitting in a certain house, that house is likely to promote a certain identity in us and when we are at our work place, just the physical building creates a identity based on the job; so too with various objects, towns, cities, and so on. Even if we go to a church or a temple, it will create within us the identity of 'i' as a Christian or 'i' as a priest.

Nothing in this physical world naturally creates in us the identity of 'I'. This leads us to the understanding of our true home or Supreme Region. If the soul is eternal and non -physical and is playing a temporary role through this body in this physical world, then whichever region it has come from onto this physical world, that region has to be at least eternal and non-physical. This is called the Supreme Region, (sometimes referred to as the Soul World). This is the only region that does not remind us of various false identities. When we see ourselves in this region, we see ourselves as souls' - beings of light, eternal, peaceful, compassionate and carefree.

This region does not tell us that we are male or female, young or old bodies, nor does it remind us of the job or status. Neither are we reminded of the various circumstances or relationships, or problems of this world. Just the thought of our true home reminds us very clearly of who we are and helps us to understand with greater clarity the transitory nature of the body and the various roles that we play through the body. The Supreme Region is also the abode of the Supreme Being, so we can go a step further and see ourselves as beings of light in our Supreme Region with the Supreme Being, and this experience will give the maximum chance for the 'I' identity to grow.

Meditation

During this practice, I use my divine vision or the third eye to see and experience the truth.

I see my self as a bodiless being... a being of light, apart from this body ... I own nothing... I can lose nothing... I am secure and carefree... I experience peace and compassion.

Now, I see myself in my home... the Supreme Region. I see myself as a peaceful being of light in a vast expanse of golden red light... a world of peace... I am immersed in peace.

In my home, I find myself in the company of my Supreme Father... I feel that I am accepted as I am, and what I am... I am loved as a very dear child... I am seen with respect, as equal... I am seen with my original and highest qualities... His company reminds me of my highest qualities... I see His greatness, I sense His peace... I am showered by His love... I see Him as my close companion and friend... I feel I have found everything.

The identity and its Entourage

So far, we have seen how the identity affects our thoughts and vision. In fact, the identity has a lot greater influence. Each and every identity has its own: a) attitude; b) emotional state(s); c) thoughts; d) vision; e) actions; and f) priorities.

Thus, when a person is in an identity of a successful businessman, during those moments, his attitude will be one of making extra profits. He will have a certain range of emotions, such as anxiety, stress, etc., depending upon the state of his business. His thoughts will be on business, banks and clients and his vision will also be tainted by his business. For example, if he were to see some stones, he would probably see them for their present value in the market! His priorities and actions would also be in business. Sometime later, as the identity changes, the same person will have different attitudes, emotions, thoughts, vision, priorities and actions. It is as if each identity ('I' or 'i's), has its own entourage or team members. Identity acts as a captain of the team, and the whole team operates together.

Now, if we intend to maintain the identity of 'I', we can work directly on the identity itself, as discussed in Chapter VI. We can also catch hold of any of its team members, and the rest of the team, including the identity, will be pulled in as well. We can work on the thoughts, as discussed in the chapter earlier - thoughts of the Supreme Being, Supreme Region.

We can work on the vision - see the soul in others, see the highest and original qualities in others. We can work on our attitude - one of the most precious practices is to treat the body, the different roles, etc., in third person - the attitude of detachment.

When we are in the identity of 'I', our actions are motivated by authentic compassion, mercy, selflessness, benevolence, service, joy, etc. Thus, if we were to pay attention to our speech and actions, choosing to be involved only in the actions of benevolence and service, we would then help create the highest identity in ourselves. Even the actions that may appear ordinary, like eating or washing the body, etc. can be performed with the motive of service. The body may be seen as a useful instrument for the task of service and any time spent on looking after the body will be seen as time spent for the ultimate task.

At different times, different aspects are more natural to practice. Being aware of the various manifestations of the true identity in vision and actions is useful because one can check and if needed, change. (See Figure 20.)

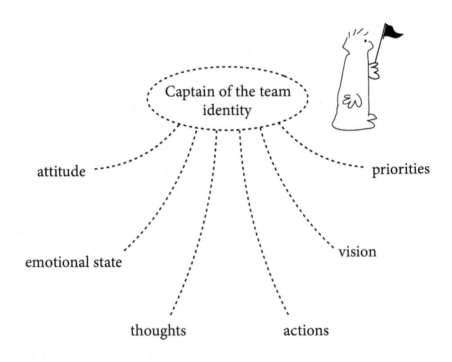

Figure 20

Chapter 7

POWERS AND VIRTUES

The Different Powers

The word power may have various physical associations, but for a spiritual seeker, that word means spiritual powers. It can be described as our ability to resist the drift into 'i' identity, or our ability to grow in the 'I' identity. In this battle between the 'I' and the 'i's, the soul needs various skills to help the 'I' identity win each time. These various skills are called powers, and some of the main ones are listed below.

The power to put a stop / to pack up

The power to tolerate

The power to merge

The power to detect / to recognise

The power to decide

The power to face

The power to cooperate

The power to withdraw

When we realise that for a long, long time, we have encouraged different 'i's to take birth, grow, and dominate our identity, and when we decide to grow in the true identity of 'I', the change will not be an instant one. In fact, different 'i's will play their games in a variety of ways, and to deal with them, one needs different powers.

Power to Put a Stop

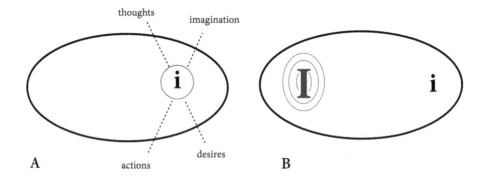

Figure 21

When we are being ruled by one of the identities of 'i', that gives rise to its expansion in the form of thoughts, imagination, desires, actions, etc. The moment we realise that we are operating from a wrong identity, we should be able to put a full stop to the entire expansion, and return to the identity of 'I'. This is seen as the power to put a stop, or to finish or to pack up.

For example, a person, while in the identity of 'i' as a businessman, may have repeated cyclical thoughts and imagination about some deals or customers. He himself may realise that those thoughts are rather useless and he would rather keep his thoughts on the

Supreme Being. The ability to stop such thoughts, imagination or action once a decision is taken is referred to as a power.

Power to Tolerate

When we are totally in the true identity of 'I', there is no experience of any form of suffering or discomfort, even under extreme provocation. The discomfort is experienced only when we are in the 'i' identity. (See Figure 22.)

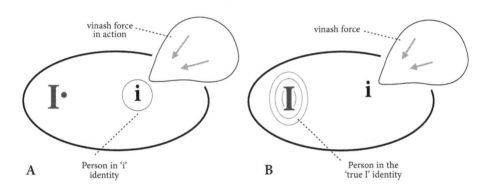

Figure 22

Under certain circumstances, if we experience annoyance, irritation, or discomfort, it suggests that we are in an 'i' identity, which is being scratched. It also suggests that we are in some way in bondage to that 'i', or that 'i' is quite dominant, and so we are not easily able to move onto the platform of 'I' identity. Normally, people immediately try to change the external circumstances to remove their discomfort. This way, 'i' is also protected. When we decide not to change the external circumstances, but to change ourselves, i.e. come into the 'I' identity, and thus free ourselves from the experience of annoyance, irritation or discomfort, then we are using the power of tolerance.

This way, we do not protect the 'i's, but that act of tolerance, along with the external unpleasant circumstances, tames the 'i', and frees us from the bondages in the long term. Tolerance doesn't imply that we have to suffer, in fact one who is in the identity of I, experiences supersensuous happiness.

We come across many opportunities for tolerance during the day - every time the circumstances scratch one of our 'i's, there is an opportunity to experiment with this power. This includes criticism, defamation, loud noises (from neighbours!) or physical pain.

To the degree we tolerate the situation from 'I' identity, we break the past bondages with those 'i's and we experience freedom.

The Power to Merge (to make disappear)

When any object is thrown in the ocean, it disappears in the vastness of the ocean. The ocean won't bring it back again and again. This is seen as its ability to merge. The object still remains in the ocean, but at the same time, it is made to disappear. This is why the ocean, whilst receiving various wastes from different lands, manages to come back with clean and beautiful waves.

The identity of different 'i's bring out various thoughts, imagination, past experiences, etc. to the conscious mind. This way, 'i's are entertained, and sustained. When we come across various experiences during the day, some of them tickle some of the 'i's and at times, we bring up those experiences again later during the day or at another time, through thoughts, words or actions. This way, those 'i's are stimulated further.

The power to merge means to let those various past body-conscious experiences disappear completely, so that they do not come up again and again in the conscious mind. The various experiences do not leave impressions on the person. Just as something thrown in the sea disappears in the vastness of the sea and may not be seen again at all, in the same way, when we aim to be in the identity of 'I' all the other past experiences disappear in the vastness of time, they merge, and won't be brought up again. This power is the sign of the vastness of the intellect.

Normally, a person with many 'i's can get impressed with various experiences and once an impression is left, he will replay the experience in his conscious mind. Praise, success, pleasures in relationships, interactions, sense pleasures, people and appearances are some of the experiences which leave impressions. The person with the power to merge will be stabilised in the remembrance of the Supreme Being.

The Power to Detect

If a warrior is able to sense the danger ahead of time with whatever signals he receives, he can then take the necessary steps in advance and he would be more likely to be victorious.

One of the most precious skills which we all need to acquire is to detect the false identity in its early stages. To be able to recognise the motives behind the various actions, and the identity behind the various thoughts and feelings, is a subtle and most important power. Impartial observation by itself is the battle half won.

No one consciously wants to sustain in themselves a major illusion. The problem with the large majority is that they cannot see that there is an illusion. Those who are aware of the possible illusion and the false identities in them, need this power to spot the disguised new faces of the false identities.

For example, the one who has started with a sincere spiritual effort to grow in the identity of 'I' might switch into an identity of an image 'i' that he is a 'spiritual effort maker' and so enter into another trap of the false identity.

To the degree that we know ourselves, to that degree we should be able to detect the motives, feelings, the identity, and the needs of others who are in front of us.

The Power to Decide

We often come across a situation where we have a choice of two different actions. We may be quite clear as to which action is in the right identity, and which one is from the wrong identity. There may be the past habit of doing the wrong action as well. In that situation, to restrain from the wrong action and to decide in favour of the right action and to implement that action, is considered to be a power.

To give a simple example, a person might have decided to rise at a certain time. At the right time, the identity of 'i' will suggest to stay in bed a little longer because of various clever reasons. The one who succumbs to these suggestions lacks the power to decide and the one who implements his decision grows in that power.

At different times, once we detect that our identity is a false identity, we need power to take a decision to change the identity and further to implement the decision. It is our ability to exert our 'will'. Once we change ourselves to true identity, our thoughts, words, motives and actions also change.

The Power to Face

Even though our aim is to be free from the support of the physical world for our inner needs, we do not aim to stay away from the objects of the physical world. It is said, 'Those who run away from the objects of lust and greed, may take lust and greed with them.'

Our aim is to stay within this world, amongst the objects of the senses and positions of arrogance, yet be strong enough in the identity of 'I' not to be pulled into any of the body-conscious false identities. (See Figure 23.)

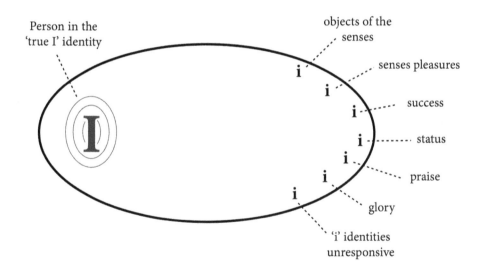

Figure 23

We mentioned earlier on, that the success, praise, glory or the objects of the senses are not our problem. It is only when we approach these external situations with the corresponding false identity 'i', that the body consciousness grows. If we approach the situation with the identity of 'I' then we do not feed our body consciousness. Also, if we approach the situation with some other identity of 'i', one that does not correspond to the external situation, then body consciousness will not grow either.

As an example, a person was at a funeral and being in the identity of a relation, was experiencing some sorrow. Suddenly someone fainted, and since that person was a doctor, he immediately had to attend to the patient, but in the process the identity shifted from the 'i' of a relation to the 'i of a doctor, and with that, the emotions and feelings also shifted in a second.

Another example is a person in a casino, who may be resting in the false identity, an 'i' based on his body or an 'i' in relation to lust. In the company of a girl, he will experience a certain pleasure and feed that particular false identity. The same person when he is at home may be in the company of a similar looking girl, but this time, he will be in the identity of a 'brother' and as long as he is in that identity, he won't grow in the identity based on the body or lust. The one who has the knowledge of the soul will choose to stay in the identity of 'I', rather than any other false identity. This ability to stay resolutely in the true identity in the face of apparent baits for the 'i's, is called the power to face.

The Power to Cooperate

Normally, when a person is under the influence of the identity of 'i's, he has his own small desires. Lots of these desires may conflict with the desires of others. Sometimes, one may be in competition with others for the same gains.

When we stay in the identity of 'I', we find ourselves free from small desires, and so free from any competition with others. We experience compassion towards others and act to cooperate and give benefit. When our actions give benefit to others but at the cost of our own comfort or physical gain, then it is described as the power to cooperate.

Cooperation implies giving true benefit. It is quite likely the person who is ruled by 'i' identities may have many desires and may need lots of co-operation. For example, an alcoholic friend may need co-operation in receiving a regular supply of liquor at your cost. Co-operation in those circumstances, if at all, will harm the other person. The absolute co-operation is to help the other person grow in the identity of 'I' and make him free from the false identities. The other person may not even appreciate the value of this co-operation at the moment, but that is the only co-operation that exists.

The Power to Withdraw

Each time we are exposed to any sense stimulation such as food, or exposed to praise, it has the potential of pulling us into one of the 'i's. In these circumstances, even before we get exposed to that potential sense trap, we need to withdraw from those 'i's and establish ourselves firmly in the identity of 'I'. This is sometimes called withdrawing the senses. Truly, we cannot withdraw our senses or abstain from sense experience. However, once we stay in the identity of 'I' and in remembrance of the Supreme Being, then the same sensations in the sense organs or the same pleasurable external circumstances, like praise, won't influence the person and so won't feed the 'i' identities. This would be called the power to withdraw in action. (See Figure 24.)

Virtues

We saw earlier that the word power is used when we move from false identities to the true identity. We know when and which

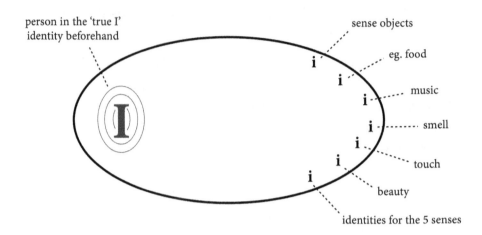

person in the 'true I'
identity beforehand

sense objects

eg. food

music

smell

touch

beauty

identities for the 5 senses

Figure 24

power we use at what time. Others may not notice this externally, and in that sense it is a very subjective phenomenon. Opposed to that, virtue is largely an objective phenomenon because it is a description by others. One cannot declare himself as virtuous! Only when others are benefited in some way, made more comfortable or happier in our company, would they describe us as virtuous. For others to be benefited from our presence, we need to be sensitive to the needs of others constantly. The needs or requirements change with time, and so we should be capable of taking different forms at different times.

For example, humour may be right at one place and time and it would be seen as a virtue. But at a different time, in different circumstances, humour may be seen as an insult and so it ceases to be a virtue. The more accurate term may be a 'virtuous state', where our presence constantly gives others the experience of benefit and gain. This happens authentically when we are in the 'I' identity. In other words, when we are in the true identity, our external manifestations under different circumstances are described as a virtue. (See Figure 25.)

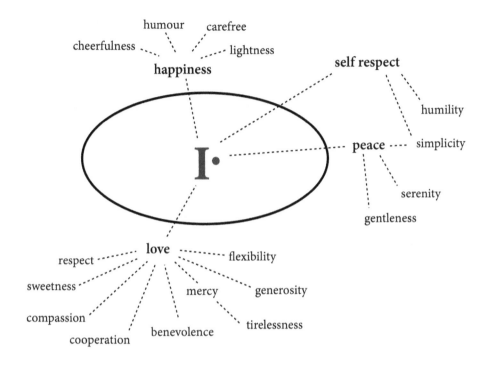

Figure 25

We saw earlier that when we are in the true identity of 'I', we experience our security, contentment and selflessness. In the atmosphere of security, our various original qualities emerge, such as peace, happiness, love, self respect, truth and honesty.

Depending upon the circumstances and environment, different aspects predominate at different times, and each of these may take different forms. These various forms are described as virtues. Thus:

· love: - from love emerges respect, sweetness, compassion, mercy, benevolence, cooperation, generosity, flexibility, tirelessness, gentleness

- peace may be expressed as patience, serenity, silence

- self-respect may take the form of humility, simplicity

- happiness is seen in the form of cheerfulness, humour, lightness, being carefree, cleanliness

- contentment is seen as purity, royalty

- honesty is sometimes seen as truthfulness

- knowledge is seen as truth and may be expressed as self-confidence, wisdom, fearlessness.

Chapter 8

THE TIME

The subject of 'creation' has intrigued philosophers, religions and science over the ages. We have many ideas on how this physical universe possibly exists, how it was created and what its purpose is. The Spiritual University has its unique insights on this subject, which will be discussed in some detail in this chapter.

In essence, it claims that this physical universe is timeless, without a beginning and endless. It solves the riddle of creation with the claim that it was never actually 'created'. In this model, souls are eternal, God is eternal, and matter is also eternal. Further, it takes a position that time is cyclical and that we go through identical repetition of cycles. These cycles are of a very short duration. In this model, history and geography are cyclical. We will see these ideas in the context of our present day beliefs and try to make rational sense, in the face of our academic knowledge.

As a preparation for this subject, we first need to know that in religions, philosophy and science there are different theories and concepts. However, the bottom line from all institutions is that 'they don't *know*'. If we want students to have open minds, we would be wiser to teach different theories, like those of Evolution and the

Big Bang, with the emphasis that these are theories and can be utterly wrong. Otherwise, as is often claimed, our present education system prevents learning.

Just to highlight the differences that exist in the Science world, we would like to illustrate one example. Professor Julian Barbour, a theoretical physicist from Oxford, in his book 'End of Time: The Next Revolution in Physics' (Oxford University Press, 2001) says, 'Based upon the present, we can never know the past'. He says the stones, the fossils, the excavations and the bones that are found, are all there in the present. To claim that all these exist now, is a scientific statement, but based on that, when we try to make history, it becomes a projection and essentially non-scientific. Hence the title of the book 'End of Time'. This is in the face of our present biology, history and archaeology, where the institution itself is based on projecting into the past, based upon the present. We often hear from historians that one can never 'know' history, all we are studying are theories and stories based upon what is observed in the present. All of this may help us to keep our minds open and be objective about the theories of time and creation.

Our Present Model

We believe that this three dimensional physical universe is made up of one set of matter. At some point this universe was created with a certain set of matter and that it is the same set of matter that changes, evolves and transforms. It may change into energy and back into matter. It is the same set that existed 13 billion years ago that continues today. It is the same set of matter which will rearrange within itself and present as tomorrow.

This model, however, has limitations. It does not explain the observations in the field of the Para-normal and psychic phenomenon.

For example, it cannot explain precognition, it does not explain miracles, and in any case, we do not yet have any explanation of the origin of this set of matter.

The New Model

In the earlier chapters, we saw the relationship between the soul and the material world, what we can call space. A unit of space is a point. Millions of points placed in a certain order make a line, millions of lines can make a two-dimensional plane, and millions of planes can make a three-dimensional space. But, the unit of all this three-dimensional space is a point. This infinite space has infinite points. The soul, the experiencer, can experience different regions of this three-dimensional space, i.e. different points of this space.

In the generally accepted model of the Universe, we believe that there is one set of matter in the Universe and that the experiencers are also part of that set. In the model of the Universe that we are proposing, the physical universe is seen as distinct from the experiencers, souls. For the time being, let us presume that all the souls are in the Supreme Region. In other words, there is no one to experience the physical world. The physical universe is not made up of one set of matter, but in this model, there are infinite sets of matter. Each set is in a static state; we shall call them stills. There is no movement in any still. Each still just exists eternally. There are an infinite number of stills. One still differs from the others stills; finer or grosser differences. There are stills with minute differences amongst them. For example, there may be a group of stills, in which the position of the entire Universe may be identical except for slight changes in the position of a bird on a tree. Within the world of stills exists all possible possibilities. In other words, all the possible permutations and combinations of matter exist in the world of stills.

It has to be emphasised again that these stills are without souls, i .e. without life and so in each still, the bodies would be identical to the static position of the three dimensional image. It may be compared to a large three dimensional slide photograph which is projected on the screen. The faces and the bodies are seen, but there is no life and there is no movement. We can represent each still by a rectangle and a group of stills would look something like Figure 28.

Figure 28

All these stills exist eternally and so all exist at any one moment. This is the extent of the universe when seen in this dimension.

The Experiencer and The 'Stills'

We know that all the stills can exist without the souls. We also know that all the souls can exist in the Supreme Region without the experience of the stills, i.e. in a state of silence. Experience begins with the coming together of the soul and the stills. Whichever still that the soul incarnates into, it will experience that still. It's as if the still is lit by the soul. If the soul was to stay in just one still, it would experience the static position of the physical world and of the bodies of that still, as we would do if just one slide was to be projected on the screen. But, from our experience, we know that we constantly experience a change, a movement of the physical world. It suggests that the soul moves or travels through the stills. As the soul enters into a different still every moment, it experiences a new scene, slightly different postures of the bodies of others and of the body it uses. It experiences a constantly changing world.

The soul obviously needs to move through the stills at a certain minimal speed to be able to give continuity to the separate stills perceived. From our experience with movie films, we know that the soul has the capacity of giving continuity to the separate slides projected on the screen. While showing a film, separate slides are projected on the screen at a certain minimal speed (25 slides per second) and the spectator, the soul, instead of seeing these inter-rupted slides, sees the continuity in the scenes and in the move-ments. From the experience of a film, the spectator may not even suspect that what he really saw on the screen was a series of indi-vidual slides.

We mentioned earlier that there are an infinite number of stills. However, we experience only those stills which correspond to the factors within the soul. Thus, the soul dictates the gross and the finer details of the still which it is to experience. The details of the body and the details of the immediate circumstances will corre-spond with the factors within the soul. At a gross level, the soul will only incarnate into the stills where there is the planet Earth with its proper atmosphere. It will also need the human body with certain senses, brain, etc. All these details match with the corre-sponding factors in the soul. This greatly limits the stills that the soul can ever experience. We see the same phenomenon in relation to space. Even though there is a vast universe, many trillion times larger than that of the Earth, a large part of it is not conducive to life - we are limited to experiencing mainly the planet Earth.

Thus in Figure 29, the path of the souls is shown through the stills. It is seen that many stills are not experienced, while the stills that are experienced are done so in a certain pattern (e.g. stills B, C, D, E, F) and with a certain speed. Both the pattern and the speed are inherent within the souls. The pattern traced by the souls is manifested externally by the apparent changes in matter. The various laws in science are essentially the study of these patterns i.e. the journey of souls through the world of stills. Since there is a relative regularity in these changes in matter, it reflects a certain discipline in the movement of the souls through the expanse of stills. (See Figure 29.)

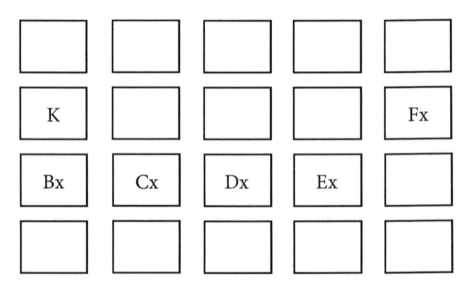

Figure 29

Another interesting phenomenon we notice here is that we human beings travel together in the world of stills. For example, if one human being is experiencing 'still F', all other human beings - 8 billion of them - are also experiencing the same still at the same moment in time and we move into the next still together. We may be experiencing different corners of that massive 'still F', nevertheless, we all remain in the same still. It is as if we are held together by a certain psychic gravity.

From our observation, we also know that from time to time, we can temporarily wander off individually into other stills, but we are soon pulled back by gravity. The so-called imagination, dreams, hallucinations, experiences under the influence of certain drugs (referred to as a 'trip') represent moving into 'off the track' stills. The stills that are experienced by a whole group together, are arbitrarily referred to as reality and the rest of the stills, (lots of them may never be experienced by anyone at any time), including those that are experienced at the individual level, are arbitrarily referred to as unreality.

We also know that we can travel back into the stills that we once experienced and it is as if we re-experience those stills with varying degrees of intensity. We call it memory. Some can travel into the future stills and experience them beforehand.

In Figure 30 our track was through the stills A, B, C, D, E and F.

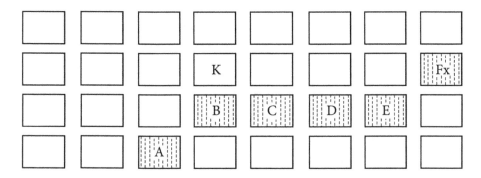

Figure 30

Our Journey Through The 'Stills'

So far, we have seen the way we human beings travel together through the stills. There is obviously a certain law that formulates the track of this travel. When we are able to realise that it is the experiencer, the soul which travels, and that even the body which is used by the soul belongs to the world of stills, it gives a very clear picture of the way things are.

There are obviously factors that dictate why the soul should experience a particular still, and also why it should travel through stills in a certain sequence, as opposed to other possible tracks. There may be many factors, but the factors that are relevant to us and which could definitely influence the experience of souls, are the 'identity' and the 'Vinash forces'. Both these factors could dictate which stills, which body and which corner of those particular stills are experienced. As both identity and Vinash forces of the souls are the variable factors, these, along with the other factors within the souls, and the souls as a group, can determine which still would be experienced at any given moment.

One wonder that we have to grapple with is that of our own eternity and the infinite number of stills that exist. If the 'Experiencer' is eternal, then there is no reason why it should ever stop experiencing the stills when its present body no longer exists in subsequent stills. If it is eternal and can be born once to experience a certain body and certain stills, why couldn't it be born twice and experience another body and different stills, as the journey of the group advances? In fact, we couldn't impose a limit to the number of bodies that one can experience.

Within this unlimited spectrum of stills there would be many, many stills which are just uninhabitable for souls. This may impose limitations on the number of stills which souls can experience. Therefore, what might start as an ambitious, unending odyssey of human beings, can be reduced to a finite and clearly marked voyage. At the end of that finite track, all the experiencers may have to withdraw from the world of stills as the further stills are uninhabitable and so they have to go back to the Supreme Region. The film is over and its time to return home.

If, in the world of stills, our journey is finite, then it is possible for us to predict more details of the beginning, the middle and the end of our journey. With the Supreme Region being our home, let us start our journey from home. While we were at home, we were in the identity of 'I' or totally soul conscious. So when we first incarnate into the world of stills we start with just the identity of 'I'. We also said earlier that our identity swings over a long period of time from totally soul conscious to totally body conscious and back to soul consciousness. Based on this information and the various observed facts, we can make a small model of our journey.

At the start of the journey, when the soul first comes into the world of stills, there are fewer human beings - all completely pure, totally soul conscious, and so, the stills, in the early part of the track are those without any 'Vinash forces'. They are of harmony, beauty, health and prosperity. We can call them 'Golden Aged' stills. As these 'beings' continue further, more beings join them from the soul world and the population gradually increases. As the journey proceeds, the tendency towards identification gradually changes with new egos being created and this influences the quality of the stills that they experience. These stills - we may call 'Silver Aged' stills. Still further, the population increases, but also body consciousness increases and the Vinash forces start to invade into the lives of these 'human beings' - thus, for the first time there are stills with Vinash forces and so war, illness, suffering, poverty etc. are seen for the first time. These stills may be called 'Copper Aged' stills. At last, when body consciousness reaches the maximum and the Vinash

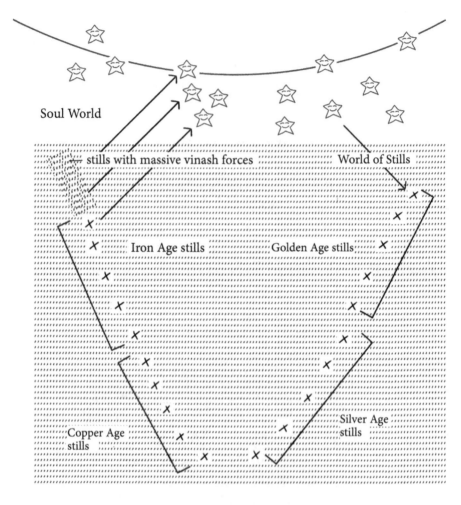

Figure 31

forces act from all directions - these may be called 'Iron Aged' stills. (See Figure 31.)

It is at this time, either because of wisdom or through pain, (stills with Vinash forces) that the soul swings back to its original soul conscious state. Being freed from the wrong identities and having achieved that original state, the soul is able to go back to its home.

We have seen that the journey of souls start in the soul world, passes through the various stills, and towards the end of the track, all return back to the soul world, thereby completing a cyclical journey. If we presume, in the absence of contrary evidence, that the factors that triggered off the present journey i.e. factors that made the soul come into the world of stills, continue to be prevalent, then they would trigger off repeated cyclical journeys. (See Figure 32.)

We mentioned earlier that the stills that are experienced are very specific to the various factors within the soul i.e. the inner state of the soul. Given a certain inner state of the soul, it will experience a specific still. At the end of one cycle through the world of stills, when the soul returns to the Supreme Region, it achieves its perfection. It will achieve the identity of 'I', the nullification of Vinash forces and the perfect inner state. There can only be one perfection. In other words, each time the soul achieves perfection, it's inner state will be identical and so when it eventually incarnates into the world of stills, it will start with the same still as in the earlier cycle. The souls from the Supreme region will also join others in the identical stills. Since the factors within the souls and in the stills are the same as in the earlier cycle, (in the absence of contrary evidence) we can presume that the cycle will be identical each time round.

Is There Progress?

We travel through the world of stills, go through destruction, return to the soul world and repeat the whole journey again identically. Automatically the question that will arise is 'where is the progress'? For the time being, let us return to the subject of the identity of 'I' and 'i's. We said that when we are in the identity of 'I', we are in a state of contentment - an inner contentment and we

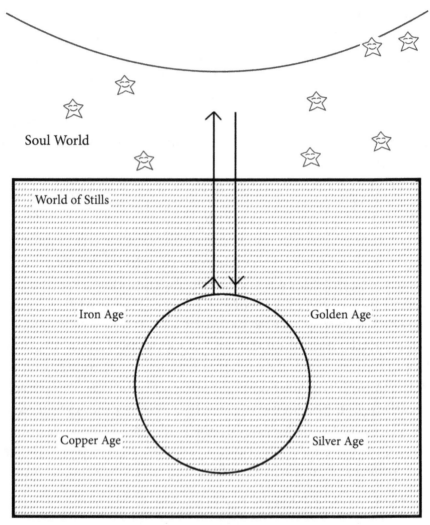

Diagrammatic representation of the cyclical journey of the 'real I'
through the world of stills.

Figure 32

are entertained by the external events. When we are in the identity
of 'i', it manifests as insecurity, discontentment and desires. For
some desires, we use the royal word 'progress'. Thus, a person
who lives in the forest may consider de-forestation and building a

city to be progress, while the one who lives in the city may consider planting trees and creating an artificial forest to be progress. The word 'progress' has been used for opposite aims at different times in history and in different cultures. It has no precise definition and is a rather 'relative' word. One of it's constant features is that the person is dissatisfied and is in an identity of 'i'.

When we experience detachment from a place, we cease to consider events around that place to be progress or a disaster. For example, we may be told that there are constant storms and earthquakes on the planet Jupiter. It won't create panic in us, neither will the opposite be considered to be any kind of progress. If we are told that the same planet goes round the sun in an identical orbit regularly, we will accept it.

We need to bring the same degree of detachment even from the characters in the stills, events and the drama cycle. We will experience great progress in stabilising ourselves in the identity of 'I' when we bring about this detachment from the drama cycle. From that identity of 'I' we experience contentment and an inner bliss, independent of the external stills. Thus we do not see any still to be progress or a disaster. Until the time we achieve that identity we need the understanding of the cycle to refine our detachment.

Some people are fortunate enough to get a glimpse of such a state during some extraordinary circumstances. Various cosmonauts, while in space, happened to get such experiences. The following is the account of one such person.

'I saw my past in front of me like a film. I was some distance away from it and the scenes were in black and white. I saw myself (the body) as one of the characters of the film. I was experiencing extreme serenity and divine calm swept through me. The time sense had expanded and I was observing the whole life in chronological order. There was no anxiety or irritation. The memory of very tragic experiences I had had was clear, but not saddening. I felt no conflict or strife.'

The Soul and The 'Stills'

Earlier, during the description of our journey through the stills, it was mentioned that the population increases because the souls incarnate from the Supreme Region into the world of stills. We also mentioned that when the souls incarnate for the first time they are free from false identities. As time passes, gradually false identities grow in the psyche and with that the Vinash forces. The Vinash force has a considerable influence on the stills that one is to experience. There will be limitation.

For a soul who is without false identities or Vinash forces, there is no limitation or bondage, so he will have a certain influence on the stills that he would like to experience. Since all the souls are held together, they experience the same stills together. The new incarnates take the driver's seat and experience the stills of their choice (consciously or subconsciously). This pattern is seen throughout the cycle, until the journey reaches the end of the Iron Age. The new souls in each generation taking the driver's seat.

All the time, the new incarnates experience the pleasant part of the still while others experience those portions of the same still corresponding with their Vinash force. This is why, at any time there will be those who are born in an extremely pleasant family and circumstances, while others are born in another part of the same planet in the midst of starvation or difficulties.

This also explains miracles or spiritual healing. Here is a new incarnate who has power in his thoughts. He wishes to see himself in a certain still, say a still with a golden ring in front of him. Since he is in the driver's seat, he moves himself into those stills and all the souls - billions of them, also accompany him into those stills. They will see the ring in front of him. All the stills always exist, so truly, it is a miracle because he could take everyone into those stills and make it into a reality.

The Lability (ability to move) of the Soul

When we study the various psychical experiences, we realise that not everyone has the possibility of experiencing clairvoyance or trance. It is as if some are more prone to these experiences than others. These are the souls who can detach themselves from the body or from the stills of the body more easily than others. We shall call this tendency the lability of the souls. Some souls may be inherently labile and those experiences may be promoted by certain circumstances or external factors. Then, there are factors like the near-death state, certain mind altering drugs, sleep etc. which can promote the lability of the souls even in those who are otherwise not prone towards lability.

The Prophecies and the Predictions

Over the centuries people have been greatly intrigued by the remarkable accuracy of predictions that were made, either during their own time, or prophecies made in the distant past that came true. There are many recorded instances, but one person that intrigues the kings, the scientists and the lay person alike, is Nostradamus from France. He was born in the 15th century and lived for less than 60 years. In his prophecies, he describes in great detail most of the important events on Earth that were to take place after his time. He accurately mentions names and numbers and at other times important clues which found place within his poetic rhythm. He speaks with the specific names about De Gaulle, Franco, and the Pasteur Institute and so on. As we can note, the events occurred centuries after his death.

The theory of probabilities may explain some immediate prediction, but the prediction such as the Pasteur Institute in Paris, which was made two centuries before Pasteur was born, is difficult to dismiss. There is no explanation for prophecies and predictions within the traditional model of the Universe. The approach that is often taken is to dismiss the observation and reject it as absurd. We do not need to dismiss these observations when seen with the model of the stills. Here we need to realise that some souls are more prone to experience predictions than others. One definite requirement would be that the soul has to be labile.

As discussed earlier, all stills exist all the time. Therefore the stills of the past and the future, the entire cycle, exist at any one moment. The souls, as a group, travel along this cyclical track. Imagine a cyclical rail track with a few passengers travelling along this track in a carriage. They see the scenes and scenery as their carriage passes through those areas. Imagine one of the passengers is able to climb above the carriage and look into the distance or, can fly around and come back to the carriage. He will be able to describe the distant scenes long before the carriage arrives there.

The soul who is labile has the ability to fly away from the gravity of the souls (the stills of the body). The one who can predict very accurately has the ability to discriminate between the stills on the track and the stills outside of the track.

Another phenomenon, analogous to prediction, is the ability of some to see from a distance. They can describe the events and scenes in the present time, but at a different place in space. It is called clairvoyance. It is a similar mechanism because the soul is labile and can move away from the pull of the body. So it travels in space, but within the same still.

Other Experiences

Over the past 50 years, more and more people have come forward to relate their experiences of the so called 'near death experience' (NDE). More than 90% of those who had NDE, relate a positive experience, while the remaining, about 10%, have a negative near death experience. Those who have a positive experience see themselves in another world, sometimes beyond their wildest imagination - they see beauty, colour, gardens, people and so on. Others see their passage through a dark tunnel. Those who have negative experiences, see a world of extreme suffering, demonic features in the beings of that world, fire, boiling liquids, frightening and poisonous animals etc.

All of these observations can be explained in the model of the stills. At the time of death, the soul is relatively labile and it may experience the same still from outside the body or may experience some other stills outside of the track. Similar patterns are seen in those who take mind altering drugs like Cocaine. These drugs possibly have the effect of bringing about a temporary lability of the soul from the body and from the stills of the body. The same is true of those who experience hallucinations. During certain phases of sleep, possibly there is a similar lability when one experiences dreams. During dreams, the soul may experience the stills which are outside of the track.

The various trance states are the experiences by the labile souls of the stills that are outside the stills of the body. In most cases, it may not be very different from a dream state, hallucinations or imagination. But, in certain cases, the soul in trance may be guided into a certain track of stills by the Supreme Being with an aim of imparting a certain knowledge. More is discussed on this subject in the last chapter.

The Independence of the Stills

We know that the stills exist eternally, so it would be wrong to speak of the age of the stills or the age of its components. Each still exists independently and is not created or influenced by any other still. 'All stills exist eternally.' So truly, the 'law of cause and effect' does not apply to the stills when seen on their own. At this stage, we need to remind ourselves that the so called cause and effect is apparent and is based on the travel of the souls through the world of stills. When we see the world with the model of stills the question cannot arise as to the cause of something existing in any particular still.

The soul travels through these different stills, so there is a sequence created of the stills experienced by the soul. Thus, in diagram 30, we will see that the soul has travelled through the stills C, D, E, F, G, creating a certain sequence. Here, to consider that the 'still D' is the cause of the 'still E', or to think that something in the 'still E' is caused by what happened in the 'still D', is an illusion. These are all independent stills. To give an example, say Mr X is projecting some slides on the screen. He shows slides at random, without intending them to relate to each other. The spectators may relate them to each other in their own mind. Later they may question as to why there is no relation between the remaining slides. They may ask what the cause was of the palace that they saw in one of the slides. They may see a certain sequence and so formulate their own law. All that it can reveal is that their model with which they explained the sequence was not true.

We approach the world of stills in the same way. We try to see the cause of whatever that exists in our own mind, and based on our own model, we try to ascribe everything we see to a certain cause. The premise is wrong. One still is not the effect of the earlier still. No component of one still is the cause of what is seen in the next still.

Thus, if we look into the sky and see that certain stars are emitting infra-red light, it provides us with the information that in these stills, stars are emitting infra-red light. It does not provide us with the information that a million years ago, that star was a thousand times larger than today and it emerged from the Big Bang explosion 13 billion years ago, or that the Universe will expand in future. Or, if we dig the earth and find some chiseled stone, it does not inform us about the age of the stone, or about the character of the person who chiseled it. All that we can say is that this stone exists in the present still. Of course there are stills with possibilities, in relation to that stone, but we do not need to explain them in our model of cause and effect. In this example, we need to see that the two stills are always unrelated. Equally, if we break our models we shall see every still independently - without relating them to others.

We saw that with the 'one set' model (traditional model) of the Universe, we can manage our day to day existence, but with that, we have been unable to explain the various authentic observations in nature. We also saw that, so far, the 'one set' model has not been proved to be the absolute model and therefore, there is no reason to prefer it to any other model. We also realised that with the model of the stills, we have been able to explain all the authentic observations that are made up to now. These include miracles, clairvoyance, predictions, out-of-body experiences, near death experiences, hallucinations, trance experiences, drug induced hallucinations, UFOs and so on. Earlier, we just gave them certain labels such as Para-normal or miracles and left them on the shelf, as if we don't need to explain these phenomena. If this model explains all the possible observations, it is more likely to be an absolute model. In any case, it is certainly a more preferable model to the 'one set' model.

With the model of the stills we will understand the concept of time as the speed of the soul through the stills. The souls, as a group, travel through the stills at a certain speed and all experience the same speed. Thus, they have a certain understanding of time. Those who have an 'out of body' experience for various reasons, sometimes relate that they experienced their entire life in front of them while others experienced a few seconds. It was as if the time was stretched out for them. To cite an example, a man fell from the 5th floor of a building and survived his fall. During those few seconds - the time taken to fall from the 5th floor to the ground floor, he saw his entire life, in chronological order and in great detail, as if he relived 50 years during those few seconds. He actually felt that he experienced a long time while others experienced a few seconds.

Some, in similar circumstances, experience their past lives, others experience their future lives (which was subsequently established to be true). The explanation for all time observations would be that the labile soul travels through a large section of a 'track of stills' at a much faster speed than others and happens to experience the stills of the remote past or immediate future.

Theoretically, it is quite possible for the soul to travel through stills backwards and thus experience time to travel backwards. Of course, all these aberrations are possible only at an individual level.

The souls, as a group, travel steadily through the track completing their cyclical journey.

We also realise that the number of days or years experienced by the souls, as a group, is independent of the Geological description of the stills. In reality all the stills are eternal and so the components of all the stills are also eternal. It is only for practical reasons or for convenience that we can describe the various entities and events with the 'one set model'. The investigation of the age of fossils, bones and so on, is done within the 'one set model', which is not the absolute model. Seen with the model of the stills, it is possible for the souls, when they incarnate for the first time, to experience the stills that already contain fossils of human bones. Thus, the time experienced by souls as a group i.e. the period of the cycle, need not be millions of years. That judgment was based on the 'one set model' and examinations of bones and fossils. It can be as low as a few thousand years.

A meditation experience
www.cambridgeinnerspace.org/med-3

Chapter 9

HISTORICAL BACKGROUND

Earlier on it was mentioned that this book has been essentially put together by the students of this knowledge. The ideas mentioned here have been personally experienced and tested and also seen to be working for many others. This book is aimed as an introduction to the vast knowledge which is available at the moment and so it may be appropriate to understand the source of this knowledge.

Around late 1936, in the north-west province of India, in the city of Hyderabad, Dada Lekhraj was leading a happy family and devotional life. It was at this time that he started to receive various spiritual experiences and periods of heightened perception which would sometimes last up to 2 hours. After one such experience, when he returned to ordinary consciousness, others close to him heard him mutter 'He was light, He was might; He told me I am to establish a new world...but He didn't tell me how!'

Time passed. Dada was not particularly preparing himself for any future role; neither did he expect any major changes in his life, but by the year 1937, the city of Hyderabad was in upheaval; thousands of local residents were receiving spiritual experiences. Some would see the physical appearance of Dada as if in a vision, others would receive his address and some would go into trance; Dada was blamed for being a magician. All the while people would gather at Dada's place, treating it as a spiritual meeting place, though Dada himself never knew what to expect. Soon he realized that when he opened his mouth to talk, he was not talking; his body was being used as a medium by the Supreme Being. Dada would listen to the new versions and concepts, to new clarity about his life and about his future. He, along with others, was listening to the Supreme Being.

The knowledge has continued to flow from that time until today. The Supreme Being would use Dada's body only for the task of speaking knowledge. The rest of the time, Dada would study the concepts, discuss with others and make effort to apply them in practical life. The Supreme Being was playing the role of the Supreme Father and the Supreme Teacher. He was lovingly called by others 'Baba' and the discourses that were given by Baba were called 'Murlis'.

The various ideas that have been discussed so far in this book are the ideas that were first introduced to us through the Murlis. These Murlis are spoken from innocence, but our own complications become a block or obstacle to our relating to that innocence. Fortunate are those who can approach this knowledge with innocence, those who can apply it in their life and reap the reward without wasting time.

In January 1969, Dada achieved his final perfection; total freedom from body-consciousness, a stage described as 'Karmateet' or the angelic stage, and from that time he has been playing a role from the Subtle Region. Subsequently, Baba continued to speak Murlis at regular intervals using the physical body of Dadi Gulzar. Dadi Gulzar left her body early in 2021 at the age 93. However, Baba's promise is that he has a part to play with us until the end of this age.

Brahma Baba

Revelation of the Cosmos

Baba only speaks the ideas and aspects that have important practical benefit to people. He does not speak aspects to impress or

those of just abstract curiosity. Those who listened to Baba right from the beginning, have many stories describing how a passing statement, often put in a certain poetic expression, came true many years later. We too had the good fortune of meeting Baba and of listening to him several times, and this has also been our personal experience. Baba can see with the clarity that others lack.

As far back as the year 1937, Baba spoke about the history and the geography of the cosmos. Perhaps when we see it with the model of the 'stills', these ideas will be understood more easily. Baba has explained that we human beings -souls - belong to the Supreme Region or Soul World which is a vast expanse of golden red light. It is a world of peace and all the souls reside in this world, in peace with the Supreme Father.

From this timeless world, souls enter the physical world. Earth is the center stage and the main planet inhabited by life. To start with, there are a few human beings and in time more souls come to the physical world. As can be expected, they all start with 100% true smriti (identity), but during a life time, false smritis gradually come into the psyche. The souls cannot leave the physical world and go back to the soul world unless they are have 100% true smriti. So the soul reincarnates into another body. But the process of entropy of the smriti continues until it is 100% false smriti. (See Figure 34.) By this time, the soul has taken a maximum of 84 incarnations.

The first phase of their life on earth is referred to as the Age of Truth or the Golden Age. All the souls are in a state of total perfection and in 100% soul consciousness. Matter is in total harmony with the souls, since there are no Vinash forces. Nature is in its highest state of beauty and human bodies are also beautiful. They are called deities.

Because of total soul consciousness, there is great inner joy, lightness, cheerfulness and love in the hearts of each one. In a gathering the individual perfection contributes towards the collective

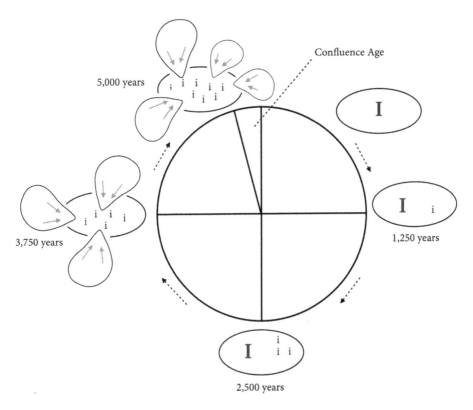

Confluence Age

5,000 years

3,750 years

1,250 years

2,500 years

Figure 34

harmony. This manifests itself as a 'dance'. There is one kingdom and people interact as one large family. The population at the beginning is around 900,000 and it gradually increases. The place is called Bharat and is located on the bank of the river Indus in the region of present day Northern India. During the Golden Age there are a maximum of eight incarnations for each soul.

As time passes and souls reincarnate, they lose their perfection yet they remain predominantly soul conscious. When soul consciousness has lost around 20% of its maximum power, the Silver Age begins. It is still a happy world; there is no trace of suffering. It is like a reflection of the Golden Age, similar, but not quite the same.

The population is much larger, with the newer souls of each generation playing more important roles than their predecessors. There are a maximum of 12 incarnations during this Age. The Golden and Silver ages together total 2,500 years. By the end of this period, souls will have lost 50% of their original power. It is as if they enter darkness after having been in light. Now the souls overall smriti is one of body consciousness. This period is called the Copper Age. All souls on earth begin to experience Vinash forces for the first time and therefore, suffering in different forms begins. For the first time there is illness and war, there are natural calamities and problems in relationships. People resort to various forms of worship and prayer, and although various prophets and scriptures appear on earth, it is nevertheless a stage of descent.

When souls have become totally body conscious and the majority have experienced extreme suffering, it is an indication that they have entered the Iron Age. The maximum number of births for souls during these last two ages is 62, and the average lifespan is short. The population increases at a much greater speed and, after a short period of relative happiness, new souls enter into body consciousness and create Vinash forces. By the end of the Iron Age all the actors are on the world stage and all are 100% body consciousness.

The illusion of body consciousness is so deep that they create systems, customs, rules, laws and theories based on this consciousness. Vinash forces bring extreme suffering on one side and body consciousness lures them into short, transitory pleasures and indulgences on the other side. Both reach their extremes during this age.

It is at this time that the Supreme Soul incarnates in the region of the planet where the souls are most body conscious and where the

Vinash forces are at their maximum. The region is the present day India.

Following his incarnation, more and more souls imbibe knowledge, understand and practise soul-consciousness, remembrance and detachment, and they become Karmateet or angelic; they imbibe powers. The large majority however, indulge in the gratification of the senses and increase their body-consciousness until the end. The aggregate Vinash forces of all these souls, brings about widespread destruction through natural calamities, epidemics and world war. The destruction will continue until all the souls leave the physical world and return to the Supreme Region. All will accompany the Supreme Soul on their return home. The Supreme Father incarnates to give knowledge and wisdom as an alternative to learning through destruction and pain, which few make use of. Those who achieve the Karmateet stage by imbibing knowledge and powers come back to the Golden Age and experience their own kingdom of peace and happiness once again.

Baba has never given a date for destruction, but a rough indication is that most of the time has passed and very little time remains. The time period from the incarnation of the Supreme Being to the establishment of the Golden Age, is called the Confluence Age. This journey from the Soul World through different ages and back to the Soul World is referred to as a 'Cycle' and the duration of the Cycle is 5,000 years. According to this model, this is the maximum period of time that any soul stays in the physical world.

It is most appropriate to commend the courage and the confidence of all the students of the Institution, particularly the early students. At a time when the entire world was talking about linear time and scientists were enthusiastic about Darwinism and evolution, these few young girls from rural India, (later known as the Dadis) confidently proposed to the world that time is cyclical and that it has duration of 5,000 years.

Fifty years on, we have cosmologists like Julian Barbour from Oxford, writing books titled 'End of Time.' We are beginning to see the obvious fallacies and limitations in the models on which science is built. Observations in the field of the para-normal, psychic phenomena, and so on, which scientists had pushed aside for a long time, have gathered a large momentum and are exposing the limitations of the present structure of science. Science may or may not be able to establish the existence of the soul or its duration of 5,000 years in the physical world, but the soul will continue to exist and the cycle will continue to turn.

We realize that with the model of the 'stills', we are able to explain all the authentic observations that have been made up to now, such as miracles, clairvoyance, predictions, out-of-body experiences, hallucinations, trance experiences, drug-induced hallucinations, UFOs and so on.

Those who have 'out-of-body' experiences sometimes relate that they observed their entire life as if projected in front of them; while others around them who were 'in the body' observed just a few seconds of time. Some people, also in traumatic circumstances, have experienced their future lives, experiences which were subsequently found to be accurate. An explanation for all of these observations would be that the labile 'Real I' travels through a large section of a 'track of stills' at a much faster speed than that of others and happens to experience 'stills' of the past or future, whether distant or immediate.

Perhaps you were not expecting to hear a message of such a radically different understanding of the self and the world, but we hope you feel that you are better off having received the knowledge of the practical steps for this personal transformation and to know that the Father of the World is here and the Golden Age is our next destination.

About the Author

Dr. Prashant Kakoday is a medical doctor based in Cambridge with a background in ENT surgery and Integrated Health. He has spent the past 35 years exploring the riddle of human consciousness. He has travelled extensively and has written on the subjects related to Consciousness, spirituality and health. He has spoken on these subjects in many countries and institutions, including the Accredited Medical Teaching Program in the USA. Prashant can be contacted via the publisher's website www.jupitarian.com.

Lightning Source UK Ltd.
Milton Keynes UK
UKHW022114120522
402896UK00007B/59